CW00471062

Bumping into BTS

어쩌다 보니 방탄소년단

Bumping into BTS   어쩌다 보니 방탄소년단

First published by Jikim Publishing Limited 2020
초판 발행 2020년 5월 15일

Authors Ji Kim, Mick Shin, Jane Do
지은이 지 킴, 믹 신, 제인 도

Editor Ji Kim | **Translation** Jun Yu
편집 지 킴 | **번역** 준 유

Design KangSaJang | **Illustration** Kain Leo
디자인 강사장 | **일러스트** 케인 리어

If you have any comments or inquiries about this book, please let us know by email below. Defective products can be exchanged.
이 책에 대한 의견이나 문의는 아래 이메일로 알려주십시오. 잘못된 책은 구입하신 서점에서 교환해 드립니다. 책값은 뒤표지에 표시되어 있습니다.

Email jikimpublishing@gmail.com
Homepage www.jikimpublishing.com

ISBN 978-1-8380192-0-4 (pbk)
ISBN 978-1-8380192-1-1 (ebk)

Bumping into BTS
어쩌다 보니 방탄소년단

Ji Kim · Mick Shin · Jane Do
지 킴 · 믹 신 · 제인 도

Jikim Publishing

무심코 집어 든 당신에게

이 책은 케이팝, 방탄소년단 그리고 방탄소년단의 팬덤인 아미, 이 세 가지 문화적 기표들에 흥미를 갖고 기획됐다. 하지만 막상 쓰려는 것은 기표 그 자체가 아닌 그 주변의 평범한 행동들에 대해서다. 저자들 모두 20대에 문화연구를 전공했지만 이 책에서 거창한 이론을 늘어놓거나 어떤 사례를 짚어 까다롭게 분석하지 않았다. 어쩌다 보니 케이팝과 방탄소년단을 영국 대학생들에게 가르치게 된 시간강사와 어쩌다 보니 방탄소년단에 빠진 출판기획자, 방탄소년단과 잠깐 일해봤다는 이유로 어쩌다 보니 이들과 책을 함께 만들게 된 예능 프로듀서가 어쩌면 팬들에게는 전혀 흥미롭지 않은 사적인 이야기를 들려주고자 한다. 그래도 괜찮다면 이 장을 넘겨도 좋다.

To those who accidentally picked this book

This book is designed with an interest in three cultural symbols: K-pop, BTS, and BTS's global fandom ARMY (Adorable Representative MC for Youth). However, what we have chosen to write about here is not the symbols in themselves, but the everyday activities surrounding them. All three authors in this book read cultural studies in their 20s, yet none of them offer here any grandiose theories, or try to subject these symbols to detailed analysis. Instead, what is offered is a collection of private stories and experiences, taken respectively from an editor who happened to fall in love with BTS; a part-time lecturer who happened to teach British students about K-pop and BTS; and a Korean TV producer who fell into this area of interest purely because she used to work with BTS a long time ago. You might not expect these stories to be very interesting to non-BTS fans, but if you are okay with that, please turn overleaf.

차례

일장.

런던에서 어쩌다 _지 킴

이장.

어쩌다 보니 덕밍아웃 _믹 신

삼장.

어쩌다 케이팝 산업 한가운데서 _제인 도

사장.

우리 함께 크리스마스

Contents

일장.

Chapter One.

런던에서 어쩌다

—

지 킴

스스로 글을 잘 쓴다고 생각한 적은 단 한 번도 없는데 어쩌다 보니 글을 쓰는 직업을 갖게 됐다. 졸업을 앞두고 전공과 관련된 기업들의 공채가 하나 둘 뜨기에 지원을 해봤는데 유일하게 합격한 곳이 잡지를 만드는 출판사였다. 지금도 그렇지만 그때도 경제 불황으로 취업난이 심각해서 전화로 걸려온 합격 통보에 1초도 고민하지 않고 가겠다고 한 기억이 난다. 돌이켜보면 그 전화 한 통에 인생이 바뀌었다. 원래 꿈은 영화감독이었는데 이게 뭐람. 10년이라는 세월이 지난 지금, 기자 일은 관두고 문화를 연구하고 있다. 영국의 런던대 중 한 곳에서 박사 학위를 받고 몇

Bumping into BTS

—

Ji Kim

I have never regarded myself as a good writer, yet somehow writing has come to be my bread and butter. Before graduating from university, I was aggressively applying for myriad jobs relating to my major, but only received one offer of a journalist position, which was with a magazine publishing company. I had no choice but to accept the offer - made over the phone - but did so without hesitation; the economy was not exactly booming at that time, and the labour market was weakening. In retrospect, this was a phone call that changed my life forever. I used to be dreaming of becoming a film director, but whatever.

10 years later on, I am researching culture and cultural production at university. I earned a doctorate from one of the colleges of University of London and have since been teaching media theory

몇 학교에서 미디어 이론과 대중문화를 가르치고 있다. 방탄소년단은 수업에서 가장 자주 언급하는 미디어 사례다. 강의 중간에 쉴 짬이 생기면 학생들이 원하든 원하지 않든 방탄소년단 노래를 틀어놓는다. 이 글은 런던에서 어쩌다 보고 듣게 된 케이팝 그리고 방탄소년단에 대한 이야기다. 싸이부터 시작해 빅뱅을 거쳐 방탄소년단을 이야기하니 약간의 인내심을 갖고 읽어주시길.

내가 박사 과정으로 입학한 골드스미스 런던대에 처음 도착한 것은 2012년 여름이었다. 공항에서 내려 우연히 동행하게 된 지인과 한인택시를 타고 한 시간 남짓 걸려 대학이 있는 뉴크로스까지 갔다. 창문에서 보이던 런던 시내의 풍경이 아직도 생생하게 기억난다.

　2012년은 영국 올림픽이 열린 해였다. 엘리자베스 여왕의 즉위 60주년이자 첩보 영화를 좋아하는 팬들에

and popular culture at several UK universities. BTS is one of the case studies I repeatedly and persistently use in my teaching. I also play this band's music during class breaks, whether or not students like it, to unwind a bit (in my defence, they mostly do). This love for BTS somehow led me to start jotting down some notes, some jibber-jabber about K-pop and BTS that I came across in London. But since this might be a little boring read for you, I shall begin my story with PSY, then move on to Big Bang, before returning to BTS. If you don't mind, your patience will be greatly appreciated.

◆

It was the summer in 2012 when I first arrived at Goldsmiths, University of London, to embark on my PhD. I took a taxi from the Heathrow to New Cross - where Goldsmiths is located - with an acquaintance whom I accidentally came to accompany from the airport. The journey took about an hour, and I vividly remember the view of London as I was watching through the taxi window.

게는 더 중요하게 느껴질, 제임스 본드 영화가 나온 지 50주년 된 해이기도 했다.

내가 런던을 상상했을 때 떠올린 것은 그런 역사였다. 템스 강을 중심으로 2천 년이 넘게 발전했다니 아무래도 고풍스럽고 운치가 있겠지. 아니지, 과거에 멈춘 듯하지만 현대적인 부분도 있을 거야. 이런 멋진 도시에서 4년이나 걸릴 (것으로 예상했던) 박사 공부를 하게 되다니 이참에 문화연구만 할 게 아니라 도시사회학 연구도 해 봐야 하지 않을까.

설레다 못해 이제와 생각해보면 기가 찬 상상을 하며 도착했는데, 내가 살게 된 런던의 동부 지역은 예상과 많이 달랐다. 학교가 있는 뉴크로스는 런던에서도 손꼽히게 범죄율이 높은 위험한 동네에 있었다. 역사적으로 영국의 노동계급과 하층계급이 거주하는 지역이었다고 들었는데 내가 갔을 땐 아프리카에서 온 이민자들이 정착해 꽤 크게 커뮤니티를 이루고 있었다. 그래서인지 거리에서 불어나 포르투갈어로 추측되는 내가 알아들을 수 없는 언어로 이야기하는 사람들도 종종 볼 수 있었다.

As we all remember, 2012 was the year of Olympics in London. At the same time, it was also the Diamond Jubilee - the 60th anniversary - of the Queen's accession to the throne; and, perhaps more importantly to the fans of spy film, the 50th anniversary of first James Bond movie. The London Olympics, Her Majesty, 007: these are the symbols I had dreamed of when thinking of London. I was especially excited to consider, 'Well, it is a city developed over two millennia around the River Thames, so it must possess some quaint historicity and old-fashioned elegance - but it is such a global city, it must also have some modern charm! Since I will be here for four years for my PhD anyway, perhaps this is a chance to branch out, and study some new and urban things, too.'

As you can see, my imagination was running away with itself. At times ambitious, at times rosy. But my vision of London as a historical capital soon subverted, by hearing a Korean song playing out across the streets. You may have guessed already what that song was - it was PSY's "Gangnam Style", which was searing its popularity across

그 와중에 날 당황시킨 건 올림픽 분위기를 느낄 겸 런던의 중심지를 찾았던 날, 길거리에서 한국 노래를 들은 것이다. 당시에 전 세계적으로 인기를 끌고 있던 싸이의 '강남스타일'이었다. 싸이가 한국 국가대표팀을 응원하는 뮤직비디오를 제작했다는 기사를 어디선가 읽은 기억이 나서 잠깐의 이벤트로 끝날 거라 생각했다. 하지만 올림픽이 끝나고도 한동안은 어디를 가도 말춤을 추는 사람들 천지였다. 주말에 모처럼 여유를 부려보자, 명화를 보고 브런치를 먹어 볼까 싶어 내셔널갤러리에 가면 갤러리 앞 트라팔가 광장에서 수십 수백 명이 모여 말춤을 추고 있었다. 그 틈에 섞여 잠깐 구경하면 어떻게 내가 한국 사람인 걸 안 건지 "안녕하세요", "나는 오빠"라며 수작을 거는 사람들도 있었다.

기숙사로 돌아가려 튜브(런던의 지하철을 부르는 애칭)를 타면 어김없이 또 그 노래가 들렸다. 상황이 이렇다 보니 내셔널갤러리에서 관광객들에 둘러싸여 몇 분 동안 숨죽여 본 고흐의 '해바라기'가 주는 감동은 잊히고 나도 모르게 '강남스타일'을 흥얼거리게 되는 것이었다.

the globe at that time. I had thought this would
be a one-off event, having read an article about
PSY making a video to cheer the Korean national
Olympics team. But even when the Olympics was
over, I could still witness people doing the 'horse
dance' here and there. For instance, my weekend
outing for brunch, seeing the paintings at the
National Gallery, sometimes involved bumping
into unexpected flash mobs of 'horse dancing'
tourists in front of National Gallery. When noticing
I was from Korea, some people would even try
to flirt with me using some basic Korean, like:
"Annyeonghaseyo" [Hello in Korean], "I'm Oppa"
[literally meaning older brother but also a flirty
way for a woman to call an older man!].

On the way back to my student accommoda-
tion on the Tube (a nickname for London's sub-
way/underground), I also got to hear "Gangnam
Style" from other sources. Somebody was always
humming it, or playing it on their phone. Sur-
rounded by these uncanny experiences meant
that my impression of Van Gogh's Sunflowers
was diluted, and instead I started unconsciously

humming "Gangnam Style" myself.

In the end, PSY's "Gangnam Style" played out across London for much longer than I had imagined. At one point, this made me want to write a paper about the consumption of K-pop in the UK and Europe, an endeavour I had no time for, as I had been up to my eyeballs preparing for my doctoral upgrade exam. Having earned a BA and MA from Korean universities, I would not say it was easy to adapt myself to the British higher education system. Generally, PhD students in the UK are admitted to universities on the basis of their proposal of research plan, and conduct the research for around four to six years. They meet on a regular basis with two personal advisors called supervisors, around twice a month, to receive tutoring and review their progress. In the second year, students are then examined by a panel of professors to learn whether they are qualified to continue their research and advance from doctoral student to doctoral 'candidate'. Luckily, I passed this exam first try, although it took me another three years for me to formally graduate. But even

이후로도 싸이의 '강남스타일'은 생각보다 오랫동안 길거리에서 들렸다. 유럽 지역에서의 케이팝 소비에 대해 논문을 써볼까 싶기도 했지만 학교의 승급 심사를 준비해야 해서 도저히 짬을 낼 수가 없었다. 한국에서 학사와 석사를 해서인지 영국의 교육 시스템에 적응하기가 어려웠다. 보통 박사 과정 학생들은 입학할 때 연구계획서를 내고 그에 맞춰 짧게는 4년에서 길게는 6년, 긴 시간 동안 이런저런 연구를 진행한다. 슈퍼바이저라고 불리는 지도교수 두 명과 한 달에 두 번 만나 개인지도를 받으며 진도를 점검받는데 2년 차가 되면 교수들의 추천으로 '박사 자격' 심사를 받는다. 4만 자 보고서를 내면 학과에서 기용한 심사위원들이 읽고 이 학생을 박사 과정의 학생student에서 박사 후보자candidate로 급을 올려줘도 될지 결정한다. 운 좋게 나는 한 번에 통과했다. 하지만 졸업을 하기까지는 그로부터 3년이라는 시간이 더 걸렸다.

이 정도도 우리 학계에서는 빨리 졸업한 편이다. 혹시 이 글을 읽는 독자 중에 영국에서 박사를 할 생각이 있는 사람이 있다면 말리고 싶다. 당신의 청춘은 소중합니다.

this, taking around five years, is considered a fair span for completing a PhD. If any of you are thinking of doing a PhD in the UK, please don't. Your time is precious.

During the course of my PhD, K-pop started to become even more popular in the UK, at least based on what I experienced. One British Hong Kongese I met declared how much a fan he is of Big Bang, one of the most popular boy bands in Korea, and how that made him eager to make some Korean friends (this detail came out while gossiping about his ex-girlfriend, who was also a huge Big Bang fan; he was pretty mad at her and was suspicious she might have taken his VIP glow stick - a cheering tool Big Bang fans use at concerts).

I sympathised with this man's outlook as I myself had long been a super fan of Big Bang's leader, G-Dragon. However, buying K-pop goods in the UK back then was not easy. When I went to G-Dragon's "Act III: M.O.T.T.E World Tour" at the Wembley SSE Arena in the autumn of 2017, I was embarrassed as a Big Bang fan to cheer without a

내가 그렇게 박사 과정을 마치는 동안 영국에서 케이팝의 인기는 더 많아졌다. 적어도 내 개인적인 경험에 비춰볼 때는 말이다. 우연찮게 모임에서 알게 된 홍콩계 영국인은 빅뱅의 열렬한 팬이라며 한국 친구를 사귀고 싶다고 말했다. 자신처럼 빅뱅의 팬이었던 여자 친구와 헤어진 지 얼마 안 됐다며 그녀에 대한 험담을 잔뜩 늘어놓다 나온 말이었다. 아무래도 여자 친구가 짐을 싸서 나간 뒤로 VIP 야광봉(빅뱅 팬들이 콘서트에서 사용하는 응원 도구)이 안 보인다며 그녀가 슬쩍 가져간 것 같다는 이야기를 할 때는 꽤 심각하게 울분을 터뜨렸다.

나 역시 빅뱅의 리더인 지드래곤을 오랫동안 좋아한 터라 그의 분노에 어느 정도 공감했다. 영국 현지에서 케이팝 굿즈를 사는 것은 그때만 해도 정말 힘든 일이었기 때문이다. 2017년 가을, 웸블리 SSE 아레나에서 열린 지드래곤의 〈Act III: M.O.T.T.E World Tour〉에 갔을 때 VIP 야광봉을 구하지 못해 빈손으로 응원했던 창피한

luminous stick, as I just could not find one here. I mean, I did see some merchants around the arena selling Big Bang T-shirts, flags and posters, but most of them were knock-offs, and no one was selling the luminous sticks produced by the Big Bang's official fan club. If his girlfriend did sneak away such a rare item, she would surely deserve his anger.

Speaking of Big Bang, they were probably the first Korean group to become popular in the UK after PSY. I am not saying this just because I am a fan of G-Dragon, but also because I remember vividly that their concerts were held at large football stadiums in London (stadiums that are used for concerts during the off-season) and yet, even so, the tickets were selling out fairly quickly. I wanted to go to the G-Dragon concert in 2017 at the SSE Arena, Wembley, but the tickets were almost already sold out by the time I started looking, so I ended up paying £223 for what was not even a great seat.

Wondering if it was mainly Korean fans in the UK who paid such high prices to see G-Dragon,

기억이 있다. 콘서트장 근처에서 '야매'로 만든 티셔츠나 깃발, 포스터를 파는 상인들을 봤지만 빅뱅의 공식 굿즈인 야광봉을 파는 이는 없었다. 그런 희귀한 야광봉을 말도 없이 가져간 게 사실이라면 욕을 들어도 어쩔 수 없다.

돌이켜보면 싸이 이후에 영국에서 인기를 끈 한국 가수는 빅뱅이 아니었나 싶다. 지드래곤의 팬이라서 하는 말이 아니라 런던 근처의 꽤 규모가 큰 스타디움(축구 경기가 열리지 않는 비수기에 콘서트장으로 쓰이는 경기장)에서 콘서트를 열릴 때마다 표가 매진됐던 걸로 기억한다. 내가 간 2017년의 지드래곤 콘서트도 몇 시간 만에 표가 동이 나 그다지 좋지 않은 자리를 223파운드(당시 한화로 40만 원)에 달하는 거금을 주고 사야 했다.

다들 이렇게 비싼 돈을 주고 지드래곤을 보러 오나, 나처럼 영국에 있는 한국 팬들이 산 거겠지, 혹 기획사가 사들인 건 아냐, 반신반의하며 갔는데 당일에 보니 관객 대부분이 현지인으로 보였다. 나와 같은 아시아 30대 여성은 뜨문뜨문 보였고 40·50대의 중장년층과 함께 온 청

I was suspicious if Big Bang's entertainment company might have cornered many of the tickets. Interestingly, however, most of the audience seemed to be local. Asian women in their 30s like myself were on the scarce side, and there were more British (looking) teenagers, accompanied by middle-aged people in their 40s and 50s. The friend who accompanied me to the concert told me it is not uncommon in the UK for parents to come as guardians to concerts and gigs with their children.

Sitting next to me during this concert was a father with his teenage daughter. He kept his arms folded throughout the entire concert, his face expressionless (though perhaps not grumpy). Overall, his attitude somewhat resembled that of my dad in Korea when he was forced (by me) to watch "Infinite Challenge" (a South Korean enter-tainment TV show). So he was making me slightly uneasy, and I kept checking his reactions over the course of concert. Soon, the performance was reaching its climax. Then, just before the final number, G-Dragon was expressing his feelings

소년들이 많았다. 함께 간 외국인 친구 말로는 영국에서
는 부모가 보호자 역할을 하려고 미성년자인 자녀를 따
라 콘서트장을 찾는 게 흔한 일이라고 했다.

　내 옆자리에도 10대 딸을 데려온 아버지가 앉았다.
콘서트 내내 팔짱을 끼고 무표정하게 앉아 있는 모습이
한국에 있는 우리 아버지가 나 때문에 〈무한도전〉을 억
지로 볼 때 같아 신경이 쓰였다. 나도 모르게 무대를 보
다가 힐끗 그 반응을 확인하게 되는 것이었다. 그러다 어
느새 공연은 절정에 치달았다. 마지막 곡을 들려주기 직
전인가, 지드래곤이 그날 공연에 대한 소감을 밝히다 문
득 앞으로 몇 년 동안은 (입대 때문에 런던에) 못 올지도 모르
겠다고 말했다. 나도 모르게 그 말에 눈시울이 뜨거워졌
다. 아무래도 10대 팬들 사이에서 울 수는 없으니까 복받
치는 감정을 억누르려 애썼다. 그런데 옆에서 흐느끼는
소리가 들려왔다. 역시나, 울음을 터뜨린 건 10대 팬이
었고 내 옆자리의 아버지는 그 딸을 꼭 안아주고 있었다.
여전히 무표정한 얼굴로.

about the day and saying he would not be able to come to London for the next few years (due to National Service, which is mandatory for all men in South Korea). As I listened, the tears were hot in my eyes, my chin trembling. But I tried to repress my feeling, as I could not cry in public. But then I heard somebody weeping. It was the teenage girl, and her father next to me was holding her tight, still with an impassive face.

●

Within a few months of the date of the concert, I had completed my doctoral thesis. I bound it as a book and submitted it directly to the graduate office. I felt so much better. This was so gratifying! Although I needed to take the final oral examination (called a Viva), that was still about two months away, meaning that I was left with some free time for the first time in ages. I wanted to take this opportunity to do the things I had not done before, like going to the cinema spontaneously, or watching whatever movie was on (even if it looked boring). I also visited some small galleries

콘서트에 다녀오고 얼마 안 돼 나는 박사 논문을 완성했다. 종이책으로 만들어 대학원 사무실에 직접 제출했다. 정말이지 속이 다 후련했다. 심사일까지는 2달 정도 시간이 남아 오랜만에 자유시간이 생겼다. 평소에 안 해본 걸이 기회에 해보자 싶어 그날그날의 기분에 따라 아무거나 내키는 대로 해버렸다. 영화관에 무작정 찾아갔고 곧장 시작하는 영화가 딱히 재미없어 보여도 봤다. 관광객들에게 잘 안 알려진 작은 갤러리들을 찾아가서 멍하니 앉아 있다 오기도 했다. 요즘 유행하는 노래는 뭐가 있나 유튜브가 추천하는 영상들을 이것저것 보고 듣기도 했다.

그즈음에 방탄소년단을 알게 됐다. 인터넷 여기저기를 떠도는 게시물을 우연찮게 클릭했다가 미국의 3개 음악 시상식 중 하나인 아메리칸뮤직어워드의 2017년 무대에 오른 케이팝 밴드가 있다는 것을 뒤늦게 알게 됐다. 링크된 영상을 보면서 'DNA'는 제목이 특이하게 느껴져 무슨 의미일까 궁금해 했던 것 같다. 춤을 참 잘 추네, 옷

unknown to tourists, just sitting inside to kill time. I also watched various clips recommended on YouTube to see what songs were trending those days.

Around the same time, I randomly came across BTS. For surfing the web, I accidentally clicked on a post about a K-pop group who were performing at the 2017 American Music Awards - one of the largest music awards in the USA. Looking at the attached video, the title of music video, "DNA", sounded strange to me. 'Okay, you are dancing well, dressed up well, oh and singing well live.' These were just some of the thoughts I had then. But later I started looking out for more of their songs. I also began watching dance practice clips from official BTS channels on YouTube, like Big Hit Labels and BANGTANTV, sometimes trying to mimic the dance moves. At first, I did not memorise the names of all the band members, just a few who appealed to me most, like Jimin and J-Hope, as I always admire good dancers. How could they, especially Jimin, dance so well? The dance moves were sheer magic, their bodily

을 참 잘 입네, 라이브로 노래를 참 잘 하네. 이후로 방탄
소년단의 다른 노래들도 찾아 듣기 시작했다. 유튜브에
서 방탄소년단의 기획사가 운영하는 ⟨BANGTANTV⟩,
⟨Big Hit Labels⟩와 같은 공식 채널의 영상들을 보았고,
댄스 연습 비디오들을 보면서 따라 춤춰보기도 했다. 처
음에는 멤버 이름을 다 외우지 못하고 영상에서 시선을
끄는 얼굴 몇몇의 이름만 찾아 기억했다. 평소에 춤 잘
추는 사람을 동경했던 터라 지민과 제이홉이 먼저였다.
어쩌면 그렇게 고운지, 지민이 춤추는 모습을 보면 그 손
끝에서 발끝으로 이어지는 동작 하나하나가 한지에 붓
으로 그리는 선처럼 거침없이 미끈하고 아름다웠다.

돌이켜보니 호우시절이었다. 좋은 비는 때를 알고
내린다더니, 방탄소년단도 내가 일 없이 한가한, 그래서
그들의 음악을 여유롭게 들을 수 있을 때에 내게로 왔다.
나름의 운명이었다고 믿겠다.

물론 그 시기를 방탄소년단 음악만 하루 종일 듣거
나 지민에 대한 정보를 찾아보며 보내지는 않았다. 졸업
후에 갈 곳이 정해지지 않아 걱정이었다. 어디든 갈 수 있

movements - from the fingertips to toes - finely coordinated and engaging, reminding of the spontaneous, sleek and artistic brush strokes on Hanji (Korean paper made from the inner bark of mulberry paper).

Looking back, this was a good time in my life. There is a saying in Korea that a good rain knows when to come. Just like a good rain, BTS came to me when I was finally freed from my PhD labour, and could listen to their music in a relaxed mood. I wanted to believe that meeting BTS was my destiny.

Of course, I didn't spend all day long listening to BTS songs or searching for information about Jimin. I was concerned about being unemployed after my graduation, and was willing to go anywhere there was a job. But nobody offered me one, and failing a few job interviews made things even worse, making me feel ashamed of myself. Thinking back, I don't think I did anything wrong, but it certainly felt like it did.

In this state, I could not really enjoy any day fully. My life was going along, but I could not

었지만 어디서도 불러주지 않더라고. 어렵게 올라간 최종 인터뷰에서 몇 번이나 떨어지자 괜히 내 자신이 한심했다. 사실 내가 잘못한 건 없는데 왜 그랬을까.

그러다 보니 어떤 하루도 완전히, 완벽하게 즐길 수 없었다. 대체로 일상은 평온하게 흘러갔지만 불확실한 미래에 대한 고민을 떨쳐버릴 수 없어 머릿속이 어지러웠다. 그날도 그랬을 것이다. 한인슈퍼에서 라면이나 살까 해서 엔젤 역에서 내렸다. 역 출구로 걸어가는데 무심결에 통로 벽의 광고판을 봤다. 금발머리를 한 지민의 클로즈업 사진이 거기 있었다. 전문적으로 제작된 광고라고 보기엔 화질이 좋지 않았다. 사진 위에는 'Happy Birthday to Jimin'이라는 문구가 있었다. 지민이 생일이었구나. 지민아, 나도 생일 축하해.

포스터를 찬찬히 살펴보니 '지민바 차이나'라는 짧은 문구가 귀퉁이에 숨겨져 있었다. 지구 반 바퀴 돌아야 있는 곳에서 런던에 있는 사람들에게 지민의 생일을 알리고 싶었나 봐, 중국(에 있는 것으로 추정되는) 팬들의 마음이 어여뻤다. 상대가 모를 걸 알면서 지하철에서 누가 볼

shake off anxiety about my future. Simply put, I had a lot on my mind. This was probably the same on the day when I got off at Angel station to go a Korean supermarket to buy ramen (noodles). On the way to exiting the station, I noticed a billboard on the wall, with a big close-up of Jimin with blonde curly hair. The resolution of the photo was not that sharp, and it did not seem a very professionally produced advert. But the photo contained the phrase "Happy Birthday to Jimin". And I realised that today was Jimin's birthday. I mumbled, "Jimin, happy birthday", too.

Inspecting this poster more closely, I found another phrase, "Jimin Bar China" at the corner of the poster. It seemed some fans, presumably from China, wanted to announce Jimin's birthday to people in London, to the opposite side of the world. I found it delightful. It seemed to me almost an act of courage to spend so much money (assuming advertising at a popular London tube station would cost a lot) just to make a poster, without even knowing who would see it, and how it would appear to other passengers.

지 어떻게 보일지도 모르는데 그 물가 비싼 런던에서 지
하철의 광고를 사서 붙이다니 큰돈을 써버린 그 용기가
대단했다.

Some of those who were passing by me may have thought, 'What the heck is that', and considered it bizarre. Buying advertising space in an expensive city like London from the other side of the world just to celebrate a favourite singer's birthday? Some might have told their family this simply looked odd. This is just what I imagined.

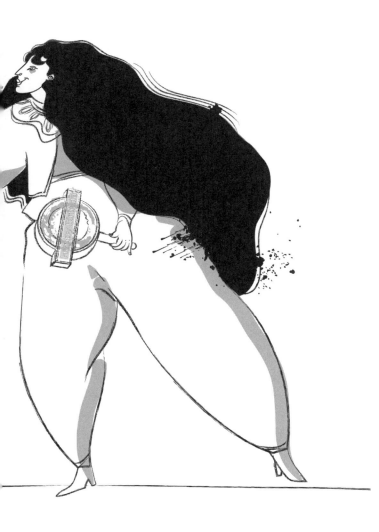

이 글을 시작하면서 밝혔지만 나는 글을 쓰는 직업을 가졌다. 보통 미디어나 대중문화를 주제로 삼는데, 생산자와 소비자를 엄격하게 구분하는 산업의 논리로서는 설명할 수 없는 사례들에 대해 쓰는 걸 좋아한다. 앞서의 생일 축하 광고와 같은 특별한 예 말이다. 문화산업론으로 따져보면 '소비자'인 팬(들)이 케이팝 산업의 상품이라 말해지는 아이돌 가수의 생일을 축하하기 위해 광고를 직접 제작했다. 게다가 자신이 살지도 않는 먼 나라의 어느 지하철 공간을 사서 붙였다. 이런 건 보통의 소비자는 하지 않는, 아니 할 수 없는 일이다. 아마도 여러 팬들이 그러한 아이디어에 공감해 후원을 하고 적극적인 소수가 직접 행동으로 옮겼을 것이다. 다시 말해, 팬들의 연대로 형성된 '팬덤'이 해낸 것이다.

　　팬덤 이야기가 나와서 말인데 석사 시절, 헨리 젠킨스의 〈팬, 블로거, 게이머〉 책을 읽고 팬덤 연구는 이렇게 하면 좋겠다는 생각한 적이 있었다.[1] '참여문화' 이론으로

As I noted at the beginning of this article, I write for a living. Usually the topics of my writing are media or popular culture, and I enjoy writing about cases that cannot be explained by a dualistic view of consumers and producers, as with the aforementioned birthday poster example. Fans are, technically, 'consumers', according to studies of cultural industries, but they produced their own goods, i.e. adverts to celebrate the birthday of an idol singer who is said to be a 'product' of the K-pop industry. They even go to lengths such as purchasing advertising space in a country far from where they live. This is not one of the usual acts of consumption. Presumably only a few took the initiative in going through with this, but I am confident that many sympathetic fans were behind this. This was a product of fandom, based on a sense of solidarity.

Speaking of fandom, when I was studying for my master's degree I had the chance to read a book by American scholar Henry Jenkins, called "Fans, Bloggers, and Gamers".[1] Jenkins is known

유명한 젠킨스는 이 책 서문에서 대뜸 자신은 "대중문화의 팬"이라며 스스로를 '아카팬'이라 부른다. 아카(데믹-)팬이라니. 학자이자 팬이라는 말일 텐데, 쉽게 말해 목사면서 승려라는 말과 다름없다는 뜻으로도 받아들일 수 있는 말이다.

그런 이중의 정체성을 갖고 있다고 연구방법을 설명하기도 전에 밝혀버리면 글쎄, '아무래도 이 연구는 팬의 입장에서 쓰여 주관적일 수도 있겠어' 하고 독자가 편견을 가질 위험이 있다. 하지만 동시에 '보통의 엄격하고 근엄하며 진지한 학자들은 알지 못하거나 혹은 말할 수 없는, 팬이어야 이해 가능한 현실적인 문제까지 다루겠네'라며 기대할 수도 있겠다.

이 글 역시 내가 글을 쓰고 시간 강의를 하며 산다고 밝힌 이상 단순한 에세이로만 여겨질 수 없을 것이다. 방탄소년단이나 그 팬덤에 대한 연구 차원에서 이 글을 쓰기 시작한 것은 결코 아니었지만 내 과거의 경험이나 직업적 특수성이 글 내용에 반영되지 않을 리도 없다. 이 글을 어떤 아카팬의 글로 봐도 무방할 것이다.

for his theory of "participatory culture", and for identifying himself as an "Acafan of popular culture", that is, an academic who self-identifies as a member of fandom. Does this make sense? It might sound as absurd as being a pastor and a monk at the same time, but I thought I should do my research in the same fashion.

If you reveal this kind of double identity from the outset, before explaining your research method, well, there is a chance your research may be misunderstood as lacking academic rigour and objectivity, or just being too subjective. At the same time, however, your work may be able to deal with real "fan problems" that typical strict, stern, serious, outsider scholars might not consider.

What about this very essay? As I write and lecture at universities for my living, some may take this piece of writing to be more than just a layman's essay. In a sense, I am one of the "Acafans", too. But let me be absolutely clear: I did NOT start writing this as a means to research BTS, BTS fandom or K-pop. All in all, this is a record of my personal history and feelings, a record I started

젠킨스로 돌아가, 팬덤에 대한 그의 주장에서 내가 동의하는 부분이 있어 짧게 소개하고자 한다. 젠킨스는 〈스타트렉〉 시리즈의 팬들이 할리우드가 기획하고 생산하는 상품을 수동적으로 소비하는 것에 만족하지 않고 팬진과 같은 2차 저작물 생산을 통해 그 상품의 문화적 의미를 새롭게 재구성하는 모습을 보고 이들을 단순한 소비자로 여길 수 없다고 주장했다. 산업의 의도와 무관한 활동을 주체적으로 해냈다는 점에서 이들은 능동성을 갖춘 창의집단으로 불려야 한다는 것이다.

보통 '아미'로 불리는 방탄소년단의 팬 또는 팬덤의 경우, 젠킨스가 말한 그런 사례가 정말 너무 많다. 어쩌다 보니 알게 된 사례들만 정리해도 몇 달은 걸릴 듯싶다. 먼저 생각나는 예는 소셜 미디어에서 유명한 '네임드'('이름 난'으로 해석될 수 있는 인터넷 신조어) 팬들이다.

내 식대로 이들을 구분하자면, 기획사나 방송사가 만든 영상들을 솜씨 좋게 편집해서 올리는 '리믹서'라든지, 직접 공연장이나 사인회에서 찍은 사진이나 영상을 올리는 '오리지널 콘텐츠 업로더', 이런 콘텐츠들을 자기

making based on my growing zeal and passion for BTS over the past few years, something that is now of great importance in my life.

Back to Henry Jenkins, I would like to briefly explore some of his claims about fandom which I ascribe to. Jenkins looked specifically at fans of the Star Trek franchise, regarding them not as passively consuming the goods the Hollywood has produced, but as reconstructing the cultural meaning of these goods through the reproduction of works like Fanzines. This is how these "producing fans" are distinguished from ordinary consumers. According to Jenkins, these fans should be seen as active, creative groups, as they have made their own works, independent of what the cultural industries intended.

In this case, I think Jenkins' claim perfectly captures many key facets of BTS fandom, a group commonly known as "ARMY". It seems like there are so many myriad and diverse activities of this kind that I cannot even summarise them in an entire essay. The first example that pops into my head are the "named" fans who have become a

취향에 맞춰 선별해 공유하는 '큐레이터' 등이 있다. 어떤 팬들은 기획사가 해야 할 '매니저' 역할까지 대행해 새로운 앨범이 발매되면 웹과 소셜 미디어에서 전략적으로 홍보 활동을 펼친다. 소셜 미디어에 글을 올리는 것은 기본이고 유튜브 비디오 조회 수, 음원 판매량, 각종 뮤직 차트에서의 투표 순위와 같은 인기를 곧바로 확인할 수 있는 지표들에 대해 '총(대를 메고) 공(격)'을 하기도 한다. 이런 '네임드' 팬들은 어떤 콘텐츠가 팬들 사이에서 공유되는지에 영향을 미친다는 점에서 과거 매스미디어가 독점하다시피 했던 취향을 제조하는 문화매개자 역할을 한다고 볼 수도 있다.

그런데 내가 엔젤 역에서 본 지하철 전광판 광고의 경우에는 조금 다른 경우다. 앞서도 밝혔듯이 개인이 아닌 집단으로서의 팬, 팬덤이 한 일이기 때문이다. 나중에 찾아보니 실제로 포스터에 쓰여 있던 '지민바 차이나'는 지민의 중국 팬클럽 이름이었다. 그해 10월에 있는 지민의 생일을 기념해 이들은 전 세계 각지에서 주최하는 '짐토버'(영어로 지민과 10월을 합성한 단어) 축하 이벤트를 벌였

kind of social media "influencer" through their love of BTS.

From what I have seen, there are a few different categories of these "named" fans: such as "remixers" who deftly edit and rework the video clips from K-pop companies or broadcasters and upload them online; "original content uploaders", who post a number of original photos or videos they themselves have taken at concerts or events; "curators" who single out, rearrange and share those user-generated content in accordance with certain themes. Some fans even act as "managers" for their loved K-pop groups, for instance, by strategically promoting them on the web and social media upon release of every new album. This includes not only simply posting on social media, but also participating in what they call a "total attack [together to hit]", that is, sparing no effort to increase their popularity, from YouTube video views and album sales, to vote rankings on almost all kinds of music charts in Korea. These "named" fans thus exert some influence over what content is popular and what is circulated among fans,

고 내가 간 런던 엔젤 역뿐 아니라 미국 뉴욕의 타임즈 스퀘어와 네덜란드 암스테르담의 지고 돔에서도 전광판을 이용해 광고를 게시했다.[2]

혹시나 싶어 찾아보니 역시나 2019년에도 비슷한 이벤트가 이어졌다. 중국 45개 도시에서 무려 318개에 달하는 극장들의 LCD 스크린을 빌려 광고를 했다. 서울 지하철 4호선을 지나는 한 열차를 통째로 빌려 지민의 이미지로 꾸미기도 했다.[3]

이 지민바 차이나뿐만 아니라 다른 국가들의 팬클럽들도 광고 매체를 이용해 지민의 생일을 축하하는 메시지를 세계 각지에 흩뿌렸다. 너무 사례가 많아 이 글에서 다 열거하기는 힘들다. 국내 팬클럽인 올포지민코리아All For Jimin가 한 이벤트만 수십 가지에 이른다. 전광판과 지하철뿐 아니라 트럭과 버스와 같은 이동 차량에도 광고를 냈다고 한다. SBS와 같은 TV 채널과 인스타그램, 카카오톡과 같은 소셜 미디어의 광고 지면도 사서 직접 만든 영상과 텍스트도 선보였다.[4]

놀랍도록 적극적이지 않은가. 이런 팬(들)을 화면을

acting as cultural intermediaries, a role that used to be exclusive to the mass media, which mediated and in part engineered society's cultural tastes.

Yet the advert on the underground billboard I saw at Angel station does not seem to fall into any of the categories above. For starters, this was not a job done by an individual fan, but rather by a collective fandom. Later, I found that "Jimin Bar China", mentioned in the advert, is the name of biggest fan base for Jimin in China. To commemorate Jimin's birthday in October, they organised "Jimtober" (a compound of Jimin and October) festivals around several countries, posting adverts on billboards not only at Angel station in London but also in Times Square in New York and the Ziggo Dome in Amsterdam.[2]

Out of curiosity, I googled whether they might be doing something similar every year, and, as expected, they had organised a similar event in October 2019. The Jimin Bar China hired wall and external billboards in 318 movie theatres across 45 cities in China to put up celebratory adverts for Jimin's birthday. They also hired a tube carriage in

바라보며 감자 칩이나 팝콘을 먹는 것 외엔 큰 움직임 없는, TV나 영화의 관객들과 '똑같은' 수용자로 볼 수는 없는 것이다. 소셜 미디어에서 이들 팬 카페들이 올린 생일 축하 이벤트 제안서를 보면 생일을 전후로 세계 각지에서 연달아 개최될 각종 행사로 빼곡히 차 있다. 박사 과정을 시작할 때 낸 내 연구계획서보다 더 치밀해 보였다. 이들은 어디까지나 자기 의지에 의해 이러한 활동들을 계획적으로 한다는 점에서 매스미디어의 관객들보다 주체적이다.

게다가 이들이 만든 광고물을 살펴보면 창조적이기도 하다. 기존의 뮤직비디오와 방송영상 등 저작권이 있는 텍스트들을 재가공한 사례들이 더러 있지만 각자의 해석과 여분의 상상을 더했다는 점에서 여러 매체의 요소들을 뒤섞어 새로운 미학을 창출해 낸 '리믹스'(또는 학계에서 말하는 '미디어혼종화') 사례로 진지하게 평가받을 만하다. 적어도 내 눈에는 멋져 보인다.[5]

Seoul and decorated it with images of Jimin.[3]

Not only Jimin Bar China, but also many other fandoms in other countries use various media to spread the message of Jimin's birthday all over the world. There are so many examples of this, too many to enumerate here. For instance, there are dozens of events in a year hosted by just one fan club, "All for Jimin Korea". They have advertised not only on billboards and tubes, but also used wrapping adverts on public transport like buses and lorries. Moreover, they bought advertising space on terrestrial broadcasters such as SBS (ITV-equivalent in Korea), as well as social media like Instagram and KakaoTalk, to advertise Jimin's birthday using their own fan-generated videos and text.[4]

Isn't it astonishing how active these groups are? These kinds of fans cannot be seen as the same as "passive" couch potato types of mainstream audiences. Their proposals on social media for celebrating the birthday of different BTS members are full of incredible events. They look so detailed and meticulously planned, even more detailed

물론 세상에 조건 없는 후한 인심은 존재하지 않는다고 믿는 사람들에게는 이러한 팬들의 생일 축하 이벤트가 어떤 무형의 대가나 보상을 기대하는 활동으로 비춰질지도 모른다. 자신이 좋아하는 밴드나 그 밴드의 멤버에게서 관심을 끌려고, 또는 그러한 이벤트를 진행함으로써 팬들 사이에서 특정한 개인이나 집단의 존재를 확인 받으려는 일종의 '인정 투쟁'이 아니냐는 말도 나올 법하다. 주변의 이야기를 들어보니 팬덤 내부에서도 생일 축하 이벤트에서 큰돈이 오고 가는 것에 대해 우려하는 목소리가 있다고 한다.

팬들이 지민에 대한 순수한 사랑으로 시작한 이벤트라지만 그 사랑이 광고와 같은 매체의 상품으로만 소비된다면 오해의 소지도 없지 않을 것이다. 팬들 사이에서 과열된 경쟁을 벌이다 상업적으로 이용되지는 않을까, 나 역시 생일 축하 이벤트들을 찾아보다 걱정했다.

이러한 문제를 진지하게 연구한 마르셀 모쓰라는 인

and meticulous than my PhD research proposal! These fans are much more active than mass media audiences, planning activities voluntarily and proactively.

Many of these fan-created adverts are also highly creative. Many feature collages of images, videos, and text like music and broadcast clips that are reprocessed to avoid copyright disputes, but with an additional sprinkle of their own creativity, interpretation and imagination. These "remix" specials have their own aesthetics and could be said to deserve fair evaluation in their own right, as a case of what academics call "media hybridisation". They certainly look good to me.[5]

●

Of course, to those who are more cynical and do not believe in unconditional generosity, such fan-driven birthday celebrations may appear to be activities designed to induce some tangible reward or remuneration. They may also seem to represent a kind of struggle for recognition, attracting the attention of other BTS members, or standing out

류학자가 있는데, 한때 그가 발전시킨 이른바 '증여' 이론을 공부한 적이 있다.[6] 그의 논리는 단순하다. 선물을 주고받는 행위는 겉보기에 자율적인 것으로 보이지만 경우에 따라 꼭 그렇지만은 않다. 예를 들어 원시 부족 사회에서 선물의 교환은 하나의 의례로서 여겨져, 선물을 누군가 주면 그것을 받은 만큼 어떤 방식으로든 되갚아야 할 의무가 있었다. 이해타산을 따져 비슷한 값어치를 지닌 선물로 답례를 하면 끝나겠지, 생각할 수도 있지만 현실적으로 그러기 힘들 때도 있지 않은가. 누군가는 이 점을 악용할 수도 있다는 게 문제다. 모쓰가 연구한 원시 사회에서 어떤 권력자는 다른 사회 구성원들에게 과도한 선물을 베푸는 '포틀래치'라는 낭비적인 의례를 통해 자신의 우월한 사회적 위치를 확인하려 했다.

여기까지만 들으면 방탄소년단 팬덤이 전 세계적으로 벌이는 생일 축하 이벤트 역시 다른 팬덤과 구별짓기를 위해 벌이는 투기적 성격의 선물이 아니냐 하고 생각할 수 있다. 하지만 내 생각에는 이 경우, 모쓰의 논리로는 설명하기 힘든 부분이 있다. 그 선물의 순환이 시작되

vis-à-vis other fans. One friend of mine - ARMY of course - told me that in the ARMY some are concerned about the sums of money being raised for celebration events.

Birthday celebrations such as those described would have first started on the basis of pure love for band members, including Jimin. But when the love takes the form of public commercials for consumption, this may indeed lead to possible misunderstandings or concern. Might this not lead to an even more heated competition between fans, and might not such competition end up being exploited commercially? I was a little anxious about these possibilities myself when researching these birthday celebration events.

Around two centuries ago, there was a French anthropologist, Marcel Mauss, who studied this issue and came up with the theory of "gift".[6] I was quite fascinated by this theory. His idea is simple: giving, receiving and exchanging gifts seem an autonomous, individual act, but this is not always true. For example, in many primitive tribal societies, exchanging gifts is considered a ritual that involves

는 출발점인 방탄소년단이 가진 특수성이다.

방탄소년단이 흔히 말하는 케이팝 산업의 상품에
불과하다면 팬덤의 활동 역시 그 산업의 이해타산 논리
에 갇힐 수밖에 없을 것이다. 방탄소년단의 상업적 가치
를 더 높이는 홍보 활동으로 끝날 것이다. 하지만 이들
이 좋아하는 방탄소년단은 아이돌이 보통은 언급하지
않는 민감한 주제들을 노래하는 특이한 경우다. 이들의
노래를 살펴보면 정체성 문제로 고민하는 10대와 20대
에게는 자신을 사랑하라는 말로 위로의 메시지를 전하
고 기성세대나 사회 문제에 대해서는 서슴없이 비판한
다. 〈롤링스톤즈〉는 방탄소년단이 데뷔 이래 "한국 사회
에서 터부시되는 주제들까지 공개적으로 이야기한다"는
점에서 "K팝 기계에 대한 반감을 없애고 있다"고 말한 적
이 있다.[7]

게다가 이들은 노래로 끝내지 않고 실천으로도 옮
겨, 2016년부터는 유니세프의 아동 청소년 폭력 방지를
주제로 한 '엔드바이올런스'#END violence와 같은 사회 변
화를 이끄는 다양한 캠페인에 참여하고 있다.[8] 생일을 맞

an obligation to repay received gifts in some way. Yes, you may just return the gift with a similar value, but what if the circumstance may not allow that? What if you simply cannot afford the value and amount of a gift received? The problem is that some people might take advantage of this. In one of the primitive societies Mauss researched, a powerful figure was establishing, confirming and further reinforcing his superior social position against others through an extravagant ritual called "Potlatch", in which he gave away excessive amounts of gifts to other members of society.

So, from this viewpoint, does this suggest that such massive birthday celebrations among the BTS fandoms around the world may be a means for certain groups to distinguish themselves from other fandoms? In my humble opinion, Mauss's idea does not fully account for this, as it does not explain the specific particularity of BTS as the starting-point of the gifting cycle.

To expand on this, if BTS were purely a "product" of the K-pop industry, aimed at profit-making alone, then the fans' activities would be

이한 멤버들은 개인의 신조에 따라 다양한 사회단체들에 개별적으로 기부하기도 한다. 2019년만 봐도 리더인 RM은 생일을 맞이해 청각장애 학생들의 음악 교육에 써달라며 특수학교에 1억 원을 기부했다.[9] 제이홉은 한 어린이재단에 1억 원을 전달했다.[10] 슈가는 팬클럽 '아미'의 이름으로 소아암재단에 1억 원과 인형 329개를 전달했다. "팬들의 사랑에 보답하기 위해 기부하게 됐다"는 말과 함께.[11]

팬덤 역시 방탄소년단의 그러한 사회 활동들에 적극적으로 동참하고 있다. 생일 축하 이벤트들의 상당수도 멤버들의 이름으로 어린이나 청소년을 돕는 기금이나 자선단체에 후원하는 데 맞춰져 있다. 2019년을 예로 들면, 제이홉의 생일에 53개국의 빈민가정 아이들을 후원하는 프로젝트가 17개국 5백 명의 팬들에 의해 진행됐으며, 알려진 이벤트가 35개에 달했다. 페루의 팬들은 4천 달러를 모아 14명의 아이들이 치료를 받게 도왔으며 베트남 팬들은 1만5천 개의 공책을 선물했다. 중국과 칠레, 유럽의 팬들은 스코틀랜드의 다람쥐와 같은 멸종 직전의

intelligible through the reckoning of loss and gain. Whatever they do would be a public relations activity aimed at promoting the commercial value of BTS. But their favourite boy band is quite different from the many other boy bands and idols, in that their songs have often run the gamut of sensitive social and political issues. I am sure I don't need to explain this to the readers of this essay, or to any BTS fans, but if you look at the lyrics of their songs, they often bear strong social and political messages. They send comfort to teenagers and young adults troubled by their identity, telling them to love themselves, and are frequently critical of older customs and generations. The US magazine "Rolling Stone" once noted how BTS has been "breaking K-pop's biggest taboos" by speaking openly about taboo subjects in South Korea, like LGBTQ+, adolescent mental health issues and social pressure to succeed, raising public awareness while maintaining a respectable self-image, thereby helping to lessen some people's dislike about the K-pop engine as a whole.[7]

동물과 나무들을 살리는 캠페인에 후원금을 보탰다.[12]

지민의 생일이 있었던 2019년 10월에도 팬들의 선행은 이어졌다. 생일인 10월 13일까지 6백 명에 달하는 팬들이 서울과 부산에 위치한 대한적십자사를 찾아 혈액을 기증한 사실이 정확히 지민의 생일날에 맞춰 영국의 일간지 〈메트로〉에 보도됐다. 기사에 따르면 이들 한국 팬들은 혈액뿐 아니라 헌혈자를 위한 2천 가지의 선물들을 마련해 지민의 이름으로 의사들에게 기증했고 이들의 선행에 감명 받은 다른 지역의 해외 팬들도 혈액 기증에 참여하기 시작했다.[13] 그리고 그에 대한 답례로 대한적십자사는 팬들의 기부에 감사를 표시하며 지민에게 감사장을 전달했다. 팬들의 선물이 또 다른 선물로 돌아온 것이다.

종종 내게 있어 방탄소년단은 하나의 선물 같다고 생각했

Furthermore, the groups' activities do not end at critical lyrics, as since 2016 they have been involved in various campaigns and actions for change, such as the UNICEF's "#ENDviolence" programme, designed to protect children and end youth violence.[8] Individual BTS members also make donations, around the time of their birthdays, to different social charities. Last year, RM, the leader of BTS, for example, contributed 100 million Korean won (approx. £65,000) to a special music school for deaf students.[9] J-Hope also donated 100 million won to a children's foundation,[10] while Sugar contributed the same amount plus 329 dolls to a children's cancer foundation in the name of their fan club ARMY, noting that "I donated to repay the love of my fans".[11]

Likewise, BTS fandom actively participates in such activities. Many of the birthday celebration events are oriented around making charitable donations, in the name of its members, to children's and young people's causes. This year, for example, on J-Hope's birthday, 500 fans from 17 countries initiated a project to sponsor children

다. 취업에 대한 고민으로 힘든 시기에 그들의 음악과 활동이 위로가 됐기 때문이다. 그에 대해 어떤 식으로든 답례하고 싶은 마음에 유튜브에 새로운 영상이 올라오면 '좋아요'를 눌렀고 결국엔 이 책까지 만들게 됐다. 내 경우 역시 방탄소년단 음악이 촉발한 선물의 순환 사례라 할 것이다.

이처럼 방탄소년단 주변에는 너무 다양한 선물이 순환하고 있어 그 성질을 하나로 뭉뚱그려 설명할 수 없어 보인다. 개중에는 분명 과시를 위한 소모적인 활동도 있을 것이다. 하지만 기부처럼 타인에 대한 사랑, 혹은 약자에 대한 존중과 관대함과 같은 인본주의적 가치에 의미를 둔 활동도 있다. 그렇다고 이 글을 이럴 수도 있고, 저럴 수도 있다는 식의 양비론으로 끝내고 싶진 않다.

확실한 건 방탄소년단과 팬덤 사이의 선물의 교환은 본질적으로 사랑이라는 정서적인 동기로부터 이끌어진다는 것이다. 사랑하는 상대를 실망시키고 싶지 않은 건 인간의 본능이 아닐까. 나는 방탄소년단에게 자랑이 될 만한 팬이 되고 싶고 다른 팬들도 나와 같은 마음일 것이라 생각한다. 그래서 앞으로도 큰 문제는 없지 않을까 싶다.

from poor families in 53 countries, with 35 other similar events taking place. Peruvian fans raised US $4,000 for 14 children to gain medical treatment, while Vietnamese fans gave a present of 15,000 notebooks to children in dire financial need.[12]

Fans' good deeds continued last October when Jimin, my personal favourite BTS member, celebrated his birthday. The UK newspaper "Metro" reported that by 13th October, Jimin's birthday, at least 600 fans had donated blood at the Korean Red Cross in Seoul and Busan. According to this heartwarming article, these fans not only donated their blood but also 2,000-odd gifts for future donors, all in the name of Jimin. This encouraged other fans living overseas to participate in the blood-donation tradition.[13] As a courtesy in return, the Korea Red Cross praised the activity, and sent a testimonial to Jimin. The fans' gift gave birth to another gift.

In many regards, I consider BTS a gift for me. That is because their music and activities have offered

이제 글을 마칠 때가 됐다. 아무래도 유학 이야기로 시작했으니 요즘의 근황도 밝혀야 할 것 같다. 케이팝과 방탄소년단 그리고 팬덤이 성장하는 동안 나 역시 조금 이지만 앞으로 나아갔다. 여전히 런던에 살고, 풀타임 잡은 구하지 못했지만 몇몇 대학에서 시간강사로 일하고 있다. 미디어와 대중문화를 주로 가르치는데 지난 학기부터는 한국학 강의도 시작했다. 한국 대중문화 이야기가 나오면 수업 시간에 예시로 방탄소년단을 언급하곤 한다.

어쩌다 영국에서 대중문화와 한국학을 가르치게 됐냐고 묻는 사람에게는 방탄소년단 덕분이라고 말한다. 실제로 방탄소년단이 인기를 끌기 시작한 2017년 이후 영국에서 한국학의 수요는 기하급수적으로 늘어났다. 지금 내가 다니는 대학에서도 신입생 수가 이전보다 2배 이상 늘어나 한국 문화를 가르칠 사람을 찾게 됐다. 그러다 내가 채용됐으니 꼭 우스갯소리만은 아니다.

요즘도 가끔 한국 음식이 그리우면 엔젤 역 근처의 한인슈퍼에 가는데, 지민의 생일 축하 광고는 그 뒤로 볼

me consolation during times of hardship, as when I was anxious about finding a job. Wanting to return the favour in some way, I clicked 'like' on almost every single video clip of BTS on YouTube, and now I am making this book. No matter how exaggerated it may sound, I see this as an example of a cycle of gift-giving encouraged by the group's music.

As may be seen, there are many diverse gifts surrounding BTS, so diverse in fact that to term them all as "gifts" may be oversimplifying things. Some may actually rather be derived from an intention to show off, or something else. But there are also activities that centre around humanistic values such as love, respect and tolerance for the weak and marginalised.

I do not want to end this essay by concluding irresponsibly that some gifts are genuine and others not. One thing for sure is that the exchange of gifts between BTS and ARMY stems essentially from the emotional motive of love. This is the very human instinct of not wanting to disappoint the ones we love. I wanted to be a fan of whom BTS

수 없었지만 근처를 지날 때면 종종 그날의 기억이 떠오른다. 우연히 본 지민의 생일 축하 광고가 잠시지만 지친 일상의 위로가 됐던 그 순간. 당시엔 몰랐지만 중국 어딘가에 있는 팬들 덕분이었다. 이 글을 읽는 동안 누군가도 그 비슷한 경험을 할 수 있을까. 실은 글을 쓰는 과정에서 몇 번이나 머뭇댔다. 방탄소년단에 대해 좀 더 팬으로서, 아니면 연구자로서 쓰는 편이 좋지 않았을까. 글을 완성한 지금은 확신이 든다. 여기까지가 일단은 하고 싶은 이야기고, 끝이 아니라 시작이라고. 방탄소년단을 그리고 그 팬덤을 알게 된 후, 주저하지 않는 행동의 가치를 깨달았기에 나는 앞으로도 계속 쓰려 한다.

could be proud (even if they might never know me) and I believe other fans feel the same. So I hope the fans of the future will not interrupt this precious exchange process.

Anyhow, it is almost time to end this story, and I am worried about how to do so. As I began this essay with the story of starting my PhD, I should perhaps update a little on how I am doing these days. While BTS and ARMY have made some giant leaps in K-pop's success in the UK and around the world, I have made smaller steps in my career development. I still live in London, still don't have a full-time position, but work as an associate lecturer at several universities. I lecture on media and popular culture mostly, but from last year, I also started teaching Korean studies, with a focus on Korean media and culture. When discussing Korean popular culture, I often mention BTS as an essential case study.

To anybody who is curious about how I ended up teaching Korean studies in the UK, I say, "thank you BTS". This is half a joke, but also half-truth. The number of students studying Korean and the

demand for Korean studies in the UK has grown exponentially since 2017, the time when BTS's popularity started to soar worldwide. One of the universities I am currently teaching, for instance, saw more than double the number of freshers reading Korean, so they had been looking for someone to teach Korean culture, and recruited me.

Nowadays, I go to a Korean supermarket near Angel station whenever I miss Korean food. I have not seen again an advert for Jimin's birthday. Yet, passing by the street near the station sometimes brings back the memory and feeling of solace that this birthday advert offered me in my busy life - all thanks to some unknown fans in China. Hopefully, this essay may bring forth some similar experience in its readers.

이장.

Chapter Two.

어쩌다 보니 덕밍아웃

—

믹 신

스스로를 믹이라고 불렀더니 어느 순간부터 닉네임이 되었다. 어색한 사람이 물어오면 믹 재거를 좋아해서라고 답하지만, 사실은 16년 전 런던에서 어학연수를 할 때 플랫메이트가 지어준 미키라는 애칭을 줄여 부른 말이다. 〈'문화도시' 서울, 여행하기: 도시공간 연구와 여행 이론의 접합을 통한 비판적 문화연구〉로 석사 학위를 받았고, 도시 내 지역의 목소리를 텍스트로 엮어내고 싶다는 생각에 출판사 대표를 꿈꾸며 출판계로 흘러들어왔다.

2012년, 친구들과 함께 '우리가 말하는 우리 세대의 절망'이란 캐치프레이즈를 내걸고 독립출판 레이블 '절

Happened to be geeking out

—

Mick Shin

I used to call myself Mick and from some point on it became my nickname. If anybody asks, I tell them the name comes from my favourite singer, Mick Jagger. But in fact, it is a shortened version of Mickey, a name my flatmate from 16 years ago gave me when I was living in London. I received my master's degree in cultural studies with a dissertation entitled "Travelling Seoul as a Culture City", in which I conducted urban space research through the lens of travel theory. I then entered the world of publishing, with a hope of weaving various voices in urban spaces into texts, and with a dream of one day becoming the CEO of a major publisher.

In 2012, with some friends I then established an independent publication company called "Despair Books" in Korea, under the catchphrase

망북스'를 만들었고, 퇴직금을 털어 만든 피눈물 흡혈 잡지 〈사표: 첫 사표〉를 발행했다. 런던 우범지대 여행기 〈사우스 이스트 런던에서 일주일을〉, 할아버지에 대한 마지막 기억과 유년의 추억을 모은 기록집 〈나의 할아버지는 제주〉를 쓰고 만들었다. 현재 출판사 대표는 되지 못했고 평범한 편집자로 일한다. 좋아하는 것은 방탄소년단이고 취미는 방탄소년단 덕질하기다. 이제부터 나의 짧고 굵은 덕질사를 풀어보려 한다.

나는 늦덕이다. 덕질판에서는 아티스트가 데뷔한 초기에 덕질을 시작한 팬을 '입덕', 데뷔 후 한참이 지나서 팬이 된 사람을 '늦덕'이라고 한다. 2017년 말에 관심을 가지기 시작해 2018년 초 팬덤계로 들어온 나는 누가 보아도 늦덕이다.(방탄소년단은 2013년 6월 13일에 데뷔했다.)

방탄소년단에 본격적으로 빠져든 계기는 유튜브에

of "the despair of our generation we want to voice". I put my entire severance fee, as well as my blood, sweat and tears into the publication of our first issue, entitled: "Resignation: my first resignation". This was followed by the publication of a few more issues, including the travel record of a crime-prone area in London: "One Week in South East London", and the personal recollection of my memories of grandfather and childhood in Jeju island: "My Grandfather is Jeju". I have not made it (yet) as a CEO at a publisher of any description, and I am still working as an ordinary book editor somewhere. But what I love is BTS, and my favourite hobby is geeking out on this amazing band. This essay therefore describes the unfolding of my short yet intense history as a fangirl.

●

I am a "Neut-deok". In the world of fandom in Korea, this term refers to a fan who got into the fandom late, long after the initial debut of the group. I started getting into BTS around the end of 2017 and became a fan from 2018, so I am

서 공개된 다큐멘터리 시리즈 〈번 더 스테이지〉를 통해
서다.[14] 2018년 4월, 유튜브 레드 무료 이용 프로모션에
가입하면서 우연히 보게 된 콘텐츠였다.[15] 약 1년여 간 진
행한 2017년 〈Wings Tour〉의 기록을 8편의 다큐멘터
리로 만들어 유튜브 레드 가입자에게 2018년 3월 말부
터 순차적으로 공개했는데, 5월 초 최종화가 나올 때까
지 나는 틈만 나면 공개된 영상을 보고 또 보았다. 왜냐
고? 재미있었기 때문이다. 일단 영상을 잘 만들었다. '발
단-전개-위기-절정-결말'의 서사가 담겨 있었다. 시시각
각 바뀌는 월드 투어의 장소는 이국적이었다. 무엇보다
너무도 다른 멤버 7명의 캐릭터가 매력적이고 인간적이
었다. 다큐멘터리 속 그들은 귀여웠고, 웃겼고, 정말 웃
겼고, 멋있었고, 때론 안쓰러웠으며, 솔직했다. '왜 이렇
게까지 자신을 보여주지? 어디까지가 진짜지?'라는 의
문이 들었을 때는 이미 다큐멘터리에 삽입된 그들의 노
래를 따라 부를 정도로 빠져 있었다.

인정할 수 없었다. 내가 누구인가? 내 음악적 정체
성은 20대 초부터 접해온 브릿팝과 록이 만들지 않았던

definitely one of the "Neut-deoks" (BTS made their debut on 13th June, 2013).

How did I fall in love with BTS in the first place? It was through a YouTube documentary series called "Burn the Stage".[14] I happened to watch this show when I signed up for a free trial on YouTube Red back in April 2018.[15] This series comprised eight documentaries which were a record of 2017 "Wings Tour", and it was successively made available to watch for subs-cribers to YouTube Red. Until early May when the final episode was released, I watched the series incessantly. Why? Because it was worthwhile to do so. For starters, it was an extremely well-made documentary. It had a good plot, starting from exposition, to rising action, then crisis, cli-max and falling action, eventually leading to a dramatic ending. The ever-changing locations of the world tour were exotic and beautiful. Most of all, the different characteristics of the seven BTS members were attractive and humane in their own ways. They were cute, funny (really funny), cool, sometimes even pitiful, and honest.

가. 소위 케이팝이라 지칭되는 가요는 즐겨 듣지 않는다. 살면서 덕질이란 것을 해본 적도 없고 열렬히 좋아한 무언가도 없었다. 이런 내가 대체 왜 이러는 것인가? 혼돈은 그리 오래 가지 않았다. 스스로에게도 남들에게도 멋져 보일 수 있는 이유를 찾았기 때문이다.

'나는 요즘 세대의 소셜 미디어 이용 방식과 뉴미디어 산업을 들여다보기 위해 적극적으로 방탄소년단 콘텐츠를 찾아보는 것이다. 이런 변화를 알아야 1차 산업, 제조업인 출판업계 종사자로서 내 미래도 찾을 수 있는 게 아닌가? 뭐? 빅히트 엔터테인먼트의 2017년 매출이 924억 원, 영업이익이 325억 원이라고? 봐봐, 출판업계와 사이즈부터 다르잖아!' 지금 생각하면 웃기지만 그게 그때의 내가 찾은 홀가분한 대답이었다.

타당해 보이는 이유가 생기니 실행에는 거침이 없었다. 바

'Why are they showing this much of themselves? How much of is it true?' I asked myself. By the time these questions popped into my head, I was already so immersed in BTS, I was unconsciously singing along to songs from the documentary.

First, I could not approve of the fact that I was a BTS fan. How could I? I took great pride in a musical identity formed under Britpop and rock music from my early 20s. This so-called K-pop? Please. I don't generally listen to these kinds of songs. I had never geeked out on anything like this, nor had I felt so passionate about something. Why am I behaving like this? But I didn't feel lost for long. I found a good reason to like BTS and look good to myself and others. That is, 'Well, I am actively looking out for BTS contents, because I want to better grasp how the younger generation uses social media and how the new media industry works today. I need to understand these changes in order to build a better future profile for myself as someone working in publishing industry, another type of media industry. Wow,

로 유튜브 레드 정기 결제를 신청했다. 방탄소년단의 유튜브 채널에 올라온 뮤직비디오와 춤 연습 장면, 짧지만 수많은 에피소드 영상을 복습해야 하는데 광고가 거슬렸기 때문이다. 스마트폰에는 새로운 애플리케이션이 자리했다. 방탄소년단 멤버들이 직접 운영하는 유일한 소셜 미디어라는 이유로 한물간 트위터를 다시 스마트폰에 깔았다. 브이앱을 다운 받은 건 나름 충격이었다.[16] 2015년 포털 사이트 네이버가 브이앱을 런칭했을 때만 해도 '요즘 10대는 덕질도 모바일로 하는구나' 정도로만 생각했다. 하지만 그 '아이돌 방송 애플리케이션'은 내 스마트폰 홈 화면에 떡하니 자리 잡았다. 스마트폰의 애플리케이션들로 그 사람의 정체성을 판단하던 내가 말이다!

브이앱은 성스러운 '노다지'였다. 자체 제작 프로그램 〈달려라 방탄〉, 유료 콘텐츠 〈본 보야지〉 시리즈 그리고 멤버들의 라이브 방송까지, 캐고 캐도 영상은 끝나지 않았다. 알고 보니 영상 콘텐츠는 빙산의 일각이었다. 방탄소년단은 자신들만의 세계관(BU: BTS Universe), 즉 가상의 스토리를 가지고 있었고 이를 소설부터 웹툰까지

Big Hit Entertainment's 2017 sales revenue makes 92.4 billion Korean won (approx. £59 million) and its operating income is 32.5 billion Korean won (approx. 21 million GBP)? See, the scale of these operations is so different from publishing industry!'

In retrospect, I was being hysterical. But that was honestly the best excuse I could think of at the time.

●

Once I gave myself good reason to, it was not hard to start seriously geeking out on BTS. First of all, I subscribed to YouTube Red, as I found advertising irritating for binge watching music videos, dance practice scenes, numerous short episodes on YouTube channels. I installed new apps on my smartphone, like Twitter, even though I thought it was a little outmoded, purely because Twitter was the only social media BTS members used themselves. I also downloaded V Live app - this was a kind of shock to myself too. When the Korean portal site Naver first launched this app

다양한 매체로 풀어냈다. 나는 점차 텔레비전과 멀어졌다. 대신 다양한 플랫폼을 통해 게임을 하듯 방탄소년단의 무수한 콘텐츠들을 단계별로 '클리어' 해나갔다. 마치 방탄소년단이란 미디어 콘텐츠 왕국에 갇힌 듯 말이다.

그런데 이 경험이 흔히 덕질에 대해 '~카더라' 하는 부정적인 소문과 맞물려 있었냐면 그건 아니다. 아이돌에 빠져 조공을 하고 생각 없이 돈을 쓰는 '호구'가 됐다거나 정치나 사회적인 문제는 등한시하고 '오빠' 말만 맹신하는 팬은 되지 않았다. 적어도 내가 경험한 팬덤 안에서도 그런 사람은 없었다. 대신 나는 점차 괜찮은 사람이 되어가는 것처럼 느꼈다. '좋은 음악'에 대한 편견이 깨졌다. 세상에는 케이팝, 브릿팝, 록 등 누군가 분류해놓은 음악 장르가 있지만 좋은 음악은 그 카테고리를 뛰어 넘는다는 것을 알았다. 음악을 듣는 방식도 변했다. 멜론 같은 한국의 음원 스트리밍 서비스 이외에도 멤버들이 믹스테잎 공개하는 사운드 클라우드, 해외 팬들이 '스트리밍 파티'를 벌이는 스포티파이 같은 서비스도 알게 되었다.

in 2015, I just thought it interesting that teenagers would geek out on their smartphones these days. Never had I thought I would have installed that same app on my mobile, or place it on my main home screen. Can you believe I - who used to judge others' identities based on what apps they use - would do such a thing?

But the V Live app turned out to be a sacred "bonanza" - from the programmes produced by the BTS agency ⟨Run BTS!⟩ to the paid content ⟨Bon Voyage⟩ series, to the live broadcast of individual members themselves, there was almost an endless stream videos in this treasure chest. And I soon came to learn later that video content was only the tip of the BTS iceberg. BTS had their own media franchise represented as a fictional universe - like the Marvel Universe - called BU (BTS Universe) where their stories take place, and they delivered these stories through various media formats, from novels and fictions to Webtoons (digital comics). I gradually alienated myself from television. Instead, I started trawling through these myriad BTS digital formats, step by step, as if I were playing a game.

2018년부터 2019년 초까지, 방탄소년단은 더 글로벌해졌다. 2018년 5월 발표한 〈Love Yourself 轉 Tear〉 앨범을 시작으로 9월엔 〈Love Yourself 結 Answer〉, 2019년 4월에는 〈Map of the Soul: Persona〉가 빌보드 200 앨범 차트 1위에 올랐다. 2018년 8월에 방탄소년단이 〈Love Yourself Tour〉를 시작하면서 내 덕질의 시차도 바뀌었다.[17] 그해 9월에 열린 유니세프 청년 아젠다 '제너레이션 언리미티드' 행사에서의 연설뿐만 아니라, 〈굿모닝 아메리카〉부터 〈그레이엄 노튼 쇼〉까지 투어 중간중간 출연하는 해외 방송을 생중계로 챙겨보았다. 30대 한국인으로 한국 땅에 살면서 체화된 지극히 한국적이고 한정적인 미디어의 소비 방식이 바뀌었다. 나를 둘러싼 경계가 조금씩 흐려지는 느낌이었다.

다시 처음으로 돌아가자. 그래서 뉴미디어를 알게 되었냐고? 분명한 사실은 이것이다. 나는 기꺼이 빅히트 엔터테인먼트의 2018년 매출 2,142억 원, 영업이익 641억 원 달성에 티끌 같은 조력자가 되었고, 덕질을 하기 위해 출판사를 더 열심히 다니게 되었다. 그도 그럴 것이

It was like I was locked up in a kingdom of media content, all relating to BTS.

You might wonder whether my experience of geeking out on BTS was marked by the negativities that sometimes come with enthusiasm for K-pop? Hell no. I didn't become a "pushover" for BTS who spent unlimited amounts of money on BTS contents, nor a dope with blind faith in whatever BTS members were saying while overlooking all other important political and social issues. To the best of my knowledge, nobody from the BTS fandom behaved as such either. Instead, I felt I was gradually developing into a better person. The prejudice I had once had concerning what counted as "good music" was smashed. There are various music genres as categorised by industry experts, such as K-pop, Britpop or Rock, but I came to learn that good music cannot be explained fully by such arbitrary categories. The way I listen to music has also changed. I used to use Korean music stream services like Melon, but came to favour different overseas services such as SoundCloud, where BTS members would release their mixtapes,

549파운드짜리 웸블리 콘서트 티켓을 사고도 기쁨의 눈물을 흘렸으니 말이다.

2018년 말, 한국은 퀸Queen에 열광했다. 2018년 10월 31일, 퀸의 보컬 프레디 머큐리의 자전적인 영화 〈보헤미안 랩소디〉가 한국에서 개봉했고 유래 없는 흥행을 거뒀다. 어딜 가나 퀸과 영화 얘기였다. 어떤 날은 식당, 카페, 술집으로 자리를 옮길 때마다 퀸의 노래를 들었다. 인사를 할 때도, 주문을 할 때도, 계산을 할 때도 "에~오!" 하고 말해야 할 것만 같았다. 그해 12월에는 1985년 웸블리 스타디움에서 열린 〈라이브 에이드〉 자선 공연을 지상파에서 중계하기도 했다. 관객들이 콩나물시루처럼 꽉 찬 스타디움에서 프레디 머큐리가 노래하는 모습은 굉장했다.

2019년 2월, 그 웸블리 스타디움에서 방탄소년단이 공연을 한다는 티저 영상이 빅히트 엔터테인먼트 유튜브

and Spotify, where fans from across the world throw "streaming parties" for like-minded fans.

Meanwhile, from 2018 to early 2019, BTS became increasingly "global". Starting with the album 〈Love Yourself 轉 Tear〉 released in May 2018, 〈Love Yourself 結 Answer〉 in the same year's September and 〈Map of the Soul: Persona〉 in April 2019, all made it to #1 on the Billboard 200 album chart. Also, from August 2018, my geek life also went global as BTS launched the 〈Love Yourself Tour〉.[17] I watched not only the BTS speech at UNICEF's "Generation Unlimited" event in September 2018, but also virtually all the other live overseas broadcasts the band appeared on, including ABC's 〈Good Morning America〉 and BBC's 〈The Graham Norton Show〉. The modes of consuming media I had internalised as a 37-year-old Korean, a Korean-confined way of consumption, seemed to be undergoing a transformation. I was under the impression that my own boundaries were being gradually blurred.

Let me go back to the reason I started geeking out on BTS. Did I get to understand new media

채널에 떴다. 3월 1일, 나는 웸블리 티켓팅 전쟁에 참전했다. 티켓팅에 성공하기까지의 1시간 30분은 무생물처럼 감흥 없이 살아가던 내가 이처럼 무언가를 원한 적이 있었을까 싶을 정도로 간절했던 시간이었다.

5, 4, 3, 2, 1, 땡! 모니터에 영국 티켓마스터와 FA 사이트를 동시에 띄워놓고 티켓 구매 버튼을 누르기 시작했다. 방탄소년단이란 무엇인가. 무엇이기에 아메바처럼 흐느적 살아가던 나를 열정의 키보드 워리어로 만든 것이더냐. 아니에요, 제게 티켓 한 장만 내려주세요. 피, 엘, 이, 에이, 에스, 이! 플리즈!

better as a result? Well, here is an unquestionable fact: I have willingly made a teeny-tiny contribution to Big Hit entertainment achieving sales revenue in 2018 of 214.2 billion Korean won (approx. £137 million) with an operating profit of 64.1 billion Korean won (approx. £41 million). I also came to work harder at my job in order to be able to maintain my geeky life. No wonder. I shed tears of joy as I bought the £549 platinum ticket for the recent BTS concert at Wembley.

•

At the end of 2018, South Korea was going crazy over the British rock band Queen. On 31st October 2018, 〈Bohemian Rhapsody〉, a biographical drama film about Freddie Mercury, the lead singer of Queen, was released in Korea and became an unprecedented success. Anywhere you went, people were talking about the film, and Queen. Sometimes, wherever you went, from restaurants to cafés to pubs, you could not help but listen to their music. I even wondered, when ordering food, if I should say "Ay-Oh" instead. In December

2018, some Korean terrestrial broadcasting stations aired the 1985 Live Aid charity performance from Wembley. Freddie Mercury singing to a packed stadium with the audience packed in like sardines was quite a scene.

Later, in February 2019, the Big Hit Entertainment YouTube channel released a new teaser video that BTS were planning to perform at the Wembley Stadium. On the 1st of March, I entered into the Wembley ticketing war. Believe or not, it took an hour and half for me to secure a ticket. This one-and-a-half-hours was a moment of realisation that I had never wanted something so desperately as this over the course of my inert life.

5, 4, 3, 2, 1, ding! I started madly clicking the ticket purchase button on the Ticketmaster.

What does BTS mean to me? How come did it make me abandon my inanimate amoeba-like lifestyle and transform into a passionate keyboard warrior? Please, dear universe, let me have just one ticket. P, L, E, A, S, E! Please!

Long story short, I secured a £549 Wembley Platinum ticket. You know what we say when

그렇게 549파운드 웸블리 플래티넘 티켓은 내게로
왔다. 간절히 원하는 일이 일어났을 때 꼭 하는 말이 있
지 않은가. "앞으로 진짜 착하게 살게요." 착하게 살려면
고마움부터 표현해야지. 나는 티켓팅 전쟁에 함께 참전
해준 친구에게 착하게 살겠다는 말을 반복하며 참치 집
에서 착하지 않은 가격의 실장님 코스를 기분 좋게 대접
했다. 우리는 행복에 대해 이야기를 나눴다. 안정된 직장
을 다니며 차곡차곡 돈을 모아도 빚 없이 서울 땅에 내
집 하나 갖지 못하는 시대, 평생 벌어도 갚지 못할 집 담
보 대출을 받기 위해 직장이 필요한 시대, 그럼에도 집을
마련하고 노후를 한 단계씩 준비해나가는 친구들을 보
며 내심 불안했던 것이 사실이다. 언제까지 좋아하는 것
만 하고 살 수 있을까, 일한 지 거의 10년을 향해 가는데
나는 왜 모아둔 돈이 없을까, 좋아하는 것이라곤 그저 여
행을 가고 공연을 보고 예쁜 옷을 사고 맛있는 것을 사먹
는 일인데 그게 잘못된 것이었을까, 아니 내가 진짜 좋아
하는 것만 하고 산 게 맞는가. 하지만 방탄소년단의 런던
웸블리 공연 티켓팅에 성공한 그날만큼은 '정당하게 돈

something you dearly wanted actually happens - "Thank you God, I will really be a good person from now on". And if you want to keep that promise, then you should start by expressing your gratitude to the people close to you. I repeatedly said thanks to a friend of mine who also took part in this ticketing war, and treated her some expensive dishes at a Japanese-style tuna restaurant.

During the meal, we talked about the true meaning of happiness. We are living in an era when we cannot afford to buy a house in Seoul without borrowing money from the bank, even if we work hard for many years, and even if we can get a mortgage, may need to work a whole lifetime to repay it. Yet, frankly, I was anxious at how many friends of mine were getting on the housing ladder and getting set for retirement already.

This made me dwell on my geeky life. I had thoughts like, 'How long can I maintain this lifestyle? I have worked tirelessly for almost 10 years, why don't I have enough savings? I find pleasure from travelling, going to gigs and

벌어서 내가 행복한 데 쓰면서 사는 게 진짜 행복이지'라고 생각했던 것도 같다.

강렬했던 티켓팅 그 이후의 일은 여러분이 짐작하는 그대로는 아니고 티켓 수령까지 또 많은 일이 벌어지긴 했다. 어찌 했든 시간은 흘러 2019년 6월 1일, 웸블리 스타디움에 방탄소년단은 입성했다. 언론사들은 6만 석의 티켓이 90분 만에 매진됐다고 했다. 또한 그날의 공연은 브이앱을 통해 전 세계 약 14만 명이 3만3천 원을 내고 시청했으며 시청료로만 46억 원의 수익을 냈다고도 했다. 그 이튿날인 6월 2일 공연까지 합쳐 양일간의 티켓 판매로 144억 원을 벌었다고 했다. MD 판매, 브이앱 시청료까지 합하면 200억 원에서 250억 원의 매출을 냈다고 추정했다. 평소라면 어마어마한 수치에 놀랐겠지만 '양콘'을 뛰며 웸블리에 있던 나에게 놀라운 것은 따로 있었다.

concerts, buying pretty clothes and eating nice foods, but have I been wrong to spend my money on such things? Have I just lived doing what I like?' At least, however, on the day that I successfully secured a ticket to BTS London Wembley, I felt 'Well, I have been spending my earnings on what makes me happy, and I live a happy life now, so that should be real happiness'.

What followed this dramatic ticketing event was not quite as smooth as you may have expected. There were some further incidents until I actually received the tickets. But anyway, time passed, and BTS effected the entrance into the Wembley stadium on 1st June 2019. The media reported that 60,000 tickets sold out in 90 minutes. Also, 140,000 people around the world paid 33,000 KRW (approx. £21) to watch the day's performance via V Live app, making 4.6 billion KRW (approx. £3 million GBP) only the online viewership fee. Ticket sales revenue for 1st June and 2nd June together reached 14.4 billion KRW (approx. £9.2 million). The BTS concert in London, combining total ticket sales, merchandising and V

뻔한 표현이지만 웸블리 스타디움은 '용광로' 그 자체였다. 다양한 인종과 나이, 서로 다른 언어를 구사하는 사람들이 방탄소년단의 '한국어' 노래를 하나 되어 따라 부르는 모습은 충격이었다. 내 앞자리에는 방탄소년단 캐릭터 BT21 머리띠를 하고 오열하는 영국 10대들이, 옆자리에는 오직 방탄소년단의 웸블리 공연을 보기 위해 단 이틀의 휴가를 내서 인도에서 왔다는 40대 언니가 자리했다. 딸도 팬인데 영국까지 데리고 오는 건 무리라 혼자 몰래 왔다는 말에 나도 모르게 엄지를 내밀 수밖에 없었다. 한 블록 앞에 앉은 60대 한국인 부부는 조용히 응원봉 아미밤을 흔들며 노래를 따라 불렀다.

생각해보면 웸블리 스타디움으로 향하는 길도 참 이상했다. 호텔에선 '태태'(멤버 뷔의 애칭), '방탄소년단'이 한글로 새겨진 피켓을 든 10대 유러피언 소녀가 아버지와 함께 로비를 나서는 것을 보았다. 런던 지하철역에는 멤버 지민을 응원하는 광고가 붙어 있었다. 한국에 있는

Live app views, is estimated to amount to between 20 and 25 billion KRW (approx. £12.8 and £16 million). I would have been astounded by such a huge number, and I was; but what was even more astounding to me, having attended both day's concerts, was something else.

●

It may be a cliché to describe Wembley stadium as a melting pot. But as a person who flew from Korea to the UK to witness it, I was amazed by how many races, ages, and languages were there, singing along to BTS's songs in "Korean" together. Sitting in front of me were some young British teenagers wearing a headband of BT21 - BTS characters - and next to me was a 40-year-old lady who had got only two days off and flew off from India just to see the BTS Wembley performance. She said her daughter was also a fan of BTS, but could not bring her along, as that would have made it more difficult for her to travel, so she instead came in secret. I gave her double thumbs up. There was also a Korean couple, seemingly in

친구는 공연 전날인 5월 31일 피카딜리 서커스의 풍경이라며 방탄소년단의 현대자동차 광고를 보기 위해 모여든 1천여 명의 모습이 담긴 동영상을 보내왔다. 모든 것이 너무도 자연스러웠지만 너무도 이상한 풍경이었다. 현실 세계에서 목격한 방탄소년단의 인기는 SNS에서 느껴온 것, 그 이상의 이상이었다. 어떻게 이런 일이 가능한 걸까?

제일 신기했던 것은 타인의 시선에 가장 민감한 나이인 10대들이 드러내놓고 '아시안', '보이밴드'인 방탄소년단에 열광한다는 사실이었다. 서구 사회에서 가지는 아시안 남성에 대한 상을 어학연수 시절부터 목도했던 나로서는 쉽게 이해가 가지 않는 부분이었다. 아시안 남성에게 반복되어 온 평면적인 고정관념, 가령 너드이거나 왜소하고 약한 이미지는 방탄소년단에게 어울리지 않지만 말이다. '메이크업 하는 남성'에 대한 서구의 보수적이고 마초적인 고정관념도 방탄소년단의 팬들에게는 문제가 되지 않는 듯했다. "한국 남성의 피부 관리는 경쟁 문화의 산물"이라던 BBC의 2012년 기사는 2018년에 이

their 60s, sitting two rows in front of me, quietly waving an "ARMY Bomb" light stick and singing along.

In retrospect, the road to Wembley Stadium was pretty peculiar. At my hotel, I saw a teenage European girl leaving the lobby with her father while holding a picket on which the name Taetae (nickname for V, one of BTS members) and BTS written in Korean. There were various adverts supporting Jimin, another BTS members, placed across several London Underground stations. A friend in Korea sent a video clip showing more than a thousand people gathering in Piccadilly Circus on 31st May, a day before the concert, to see BTS's Hyundai Motor commercials. This looked natural on the one hand, but odd on the other. The popularity of BTS in the real world was much greater than what I had been feeling on SNS. How could this be possible?

Perhaps the most unexpected thing for me was that teenagers, who must be sensitive to each other's gazes, were going gaga over BTS, an "Asian" boy band. This was quite puzzling to me, as I had

르러 "케이팝 아이돌의 문화적 요소"로 해석되기에 이르렀지만 이러한 담론의 변화 이면에는 성별을 넘어선 '아름다운 사람'에 대한 인식의 변화가 시작된 건 아닐까.[18] 한편 '보이밴드'란 프레임은 또 어떤가. 서구의 보이밴드들의 경우 이렇게 다양한 연령, 젠더, 인종의 팬덤을 가진 적이 있었던가. 방탄소년단을 기존의 보이밴드 프레임에 가두어도 되는 것인가.

웸블리 스타디움에서의 공연을 경험한 후, 아니 방탄소년단의 공연을 보기 위해 런던에 도착한 순간부터 나는 궁금해졌다. 왜 이들은 스스로가 방탄소년단의 팬임을 숨김없이 드러내는 것일까.

seen and heard about the stereotypes associated with Asian men in Western societies long before when I was studying English in the UK. Such stereotypes were often negative and pernicious, highlighting traits such as nerdiness, weakness, and diminutive stature; although of course it is not fair to say that BTS carry any such stereotypes. Moreover, some conservative and macho stereotypical images in Western societies about "men wearing makeup" did not seem to matter at all to those fans assembled for BTS.

In 2012, the BBC published an article that the phenomenon of skincare use among Korean men was the product of a competitive culture in Korea. In 2018, the same skincare was reinterpreted as a cultural derivation of the K-pop idols.[18] But I wonder if what lies beyond such changes in media discourse is a change in the perception of beauty itself. Meanwhile, what about the "boy band" archetype? Have any boy bands from the West developed fandoms like these, consisting of such a diversity of age, gender, and ethnicity types? Can we really confine BTS to the existing "boy band"

역사의 한 풍경이 되고 싶어서 결정한 웸블리행이었다. 이 틀간의 콘서트 동안 12만 명의 타인과 마주했지만 내가 느낀 건 소속감이었다. 인종, 세대, 나이, 젠더를 넘는 초공동체가 있다면 바로 아미란 이름 아래 모인 이들일 것이다. 교과서에서나 나올 법한 뻔한 표현이 실재할 수 있구나 느낀 순간이기도 했다. 무엇이 나를 움직이게 했을까를 생각하면 그건 물론 방탄소년단이겠지만, 그 과정이 편안하게 느껴진 건 온오프라인으로 언제든 궁금한 것을 묻고, 언어가 통하지 않아도 방탄소년단을 좋아한다는 이유만으로 말을 건넬 수 있는 이들이 있었기 때문이다.

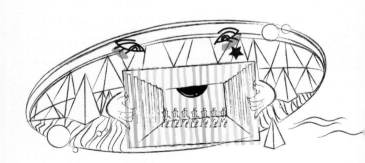

framework?

Through my experience of BTS's performance at the Wembley stadium; or in fact, from the moment I arrived in London, I could not leave behind the following question: Why do BTS fans candidly reveal their fan status?

•

For myself, I decided to travel to Wembley all the way from Korea as I wanted to be a part of a history. Over the two-day concert, I encountered 120,000 others, but what I felt over and above this was a sense of belonging. If there was a super-community that could transcend race, generation, age, and gender, that would be those who gathered under the name ARMY. This two-day concert was also the moment I came to understand the textbook expression of solidarity. What motivated me to fly to London in the first was of course BTS. But the reason I did not find the entire experience uncomfortable was because of people online and offline, with whom I could ask questions and discuss things, despite the language

우리는 '그러한 방탄소년단'을 좋아하는 사람이기 때문에 비슷한(혹은 이해할 수 있는) 취향, 가치관, 정치적 견해 등을 공유하고 있다는 전제가 깔린 소속감이기도 했다.

적지 않은 미디어가 완벽한 모습만 보여주는 스타와 이를 우러러 보는 팬이라는 낡은 프레임으로 팬덤 문화를 비춘다. 방탄소년단이 2019년 4월 컴백 무대를 가졌던 미국 NBC 〈새터데이 나이트 라이브〉 방송에서조차 팬들을 '10대 빠순이'의 전형으로 묘사하기도 했었다. 하지만 내가 이 팬덤 안에서 목격한 방탄소년단과 아미는 서로를 보듬어주는 상호보완재의 수평적인 관계이다.

방탄소년단의 전 지구적인 팬덤은 가장 한국적인 방식을 취하면서도, 지역적으로 융해되고 있으며, 때론 탈지역적인 현상으로 드러난다. 가령 방탄소년단 팬들이 해외에서 펼치는 멤버의 생일 축하 이벤트들, 즉 생일 축하 전광판 이벤트나 멤버의 얼굴이 그려진 컵홀더 나눔 이벤트는 사실 케이팝 신, 특히 아이돌 팬덤에서 흔히 볼 수 있는 방식이고, 공식 응원봉인 아미밤도 케이팝 산업에서 만들어낸 산물이다. 하지만 아미란 이름 아래 행하

barriers, just because we shared the same love of BTS. Underlying our interaction was a sense of belonging stemming from the premise that we all love BTS, so likely share similar (or relatable) tastes, values, and political views.

Despite this, many media outlets saw this fandom culture from an old-fashioned perspective, where stars and celebrities showed themselves as figures of perfection to worshipping fans. In April 2019, on the NBC ⟨Saturday Night Live⟩ show in the US, where BTS hosted their comeback gig, BTS fans were depicted as the exemplar of crazed fangirls. But to the best of my knowledge, what I witnessed in this fandom was an equal, horizontal, and mutually complementary relationship between BTS and ARMY. For instance, ARMY have participated in "Love Myself" campaigns through which BTS and UNICEF collaborate. But they have also initiated voluntary activities, made donations to charity, and even offered blood and financial donations. The fans carry out these activities under the name of BTS, but often many who attest to the activities on SNS note that they feel they are

는 봉사 활동은 팬들이 뿌리를 두고 있는 지역과 문화에 도움이 되는 방식으로 진행되기도 한다. 가령, 불 탄 아마존에 나무를 심기 위해 모금을 하는 브라질 아미, 빈곤층 어린이를 위해 멤버의 이름으로 학교를 건설하는 프로젝트를 진행한 베트남 아미 등의 경우가 그러하다. 한편 유튜브 콘텐츠로 재생산되는 방탄소년단 뮤직비디오나 공연에 대한 리액션 영상은 출연자의 언어만 다를 뿐이지, 감정과 반응을 나타내는 리액션의 방식은 탈지역적이고 오히려 하나의 형식을 띄는 것처럼 보인다. 종합하건대, 방탄소년단의 팬덤은 복잡다단한 현상인 것이다.

이 팬덤에 대해 가장 인상적인 부분은 문제가 생겼을 때 이를 해결해가는 방식이다. 과거 방탄소년단의 노래 중 몇몇 가사가 여성혐오 논란에 휩싸였을 때 이에 대해 문제를 제기한 것은 팬 아미였다. 그 방식은 정중하고도 논리적이었고 그룹과 회사 역시 이에 대해 고민하고 진심을 다해 답변했으며 달라지는 모습을 일관성 있게 보여주었다.

becoming better people in the process.

BTS fandom is undoubtedly a global phenomenon, but Korean influences are rearticulated
differently at a local level. The fandom is de-
territorialising. For example, birthday celebrations
of BTS members overseas, such as the birthday
billboard events or sharing cup-sleeves decorated
with members' faces, are long-standing traditions
in K-pop, especially in idol singer/group fan clubs.
The "ARMY Bomb", which is an official light
stick and cheering tool in BTS fandom, is also a
product of the K-pop industry. But the activities of
outreach under the name ARMY are often carried
out in ways that help local communities and
promote indigenous cultures.

Examples include ARMY in Brazil, which raises
funds for planting trees in razed Amazon forests,
or ARMY in Vietnam, who initiated a project to
build schools for poor children in the name of
BTS members. Meanwhile, BTS's music videos
on YouTube, or reaction videos to their concert
performances, seemingly take a delocalised format
despite the different languages used, with similar

2018년에는 한 멤버가 과거에 입었던 일명 '광복 티셔츠', 즉 히로시마에 원자폭탄이 떨어진 이미지의 티셔츠로 홍역을 겪었다. 혐한을 일본 보수 정당의 지지율에 이용하려는 목적이었든 어쨌든 다분히 정치적인 의도가 담긴 공격이었다고 나는 생각한다. 팬들은 단순히 분노하는 것을 넘어 각자의 방식으로 현상을 들여다보고 대응했다. 'White Paper Project(www.white paperproject.com)'도 그중 하나이다.[19] 세계 각국, 다양한 계층의 아미가 모여 사건의 개요부터 일본의 한국 침략 같은 역사적인 배경, 일본 아미J-Army의 시각까지 차분히 담아내어 홈페이지를 통해 세상에 보여주는 방식을 택했다. 이 프로젝트는 크게 알려지진 않았지만 어떤 한국 정부도 하지 못했던, 현실적이고 공감적인 반향을 만들어냈다.

우리는 지식과 토론의 힘을 믿는 방탄소년단의 평범한 팬들입니다. 우리는 학생, 작가, 공학자, 번역가, 과학자, 교사, 경제학자, 예술가, 편집자 그리고 디자이너입니다. 우리는 기독교, 불교, 유대교, 자연신교, 천주교 그리고 불가지론을 구사합니다. (중략) 한국과 일본의

ways of expressing emotions and reactions. On the whole, the ARMY phenomenon is quite complex.

Perhaps the most impressive aspect of ARMY is how they address and solve issues. In the past, some lyrics of BTS songs were caught up in a controversy surrounding misogynistic ideas. The issue was discussed in earnest on Twitter and the fans raised questions in a polite and cogent manner, and BTS themselves and their agency Big Hit Entertainment responded, after serious contemplation, with great sincerity. This has led to a more consistent approach to presenting lyrics to the public.

In 2018, one of the band members was embroiled in a further controversy and even a series of scuffles after wearing a T-shirt depicting the US atomic bombing of Hiroshima. Some conspiracy theorists on the Internet suggested that the controversy was intensified on purpose by far-right Japanese nationalist groups, to exploit anti-Korean sentiment and help boost the popularity of the Japanese conservative party. Whatever the real reason, it felt like quite a politically laden

원자폭탄 피해자들의 대답을 겸허히 받아들이며, 저희
는 모든 ARMY가 이 기회를 계기로 우리가 공유하는
가치에 대해 기억해보기를 바랍니다. 공감, 비폭력 그
리고 평화에 대한 가치에 대해 말입니다. 이는 유니세
프 #ENDviolence 캠페인을 지지하는 방탄소년단의
LOVE MYSELF 캠페인과 같은 맥락에 있습니다.

- White Paper Project 홈페이지에서 발췌

2019년 10월 29일, 서울에서 열린 〈Love Yourself:
Speak Yourself〉 더 파이널 콘서트에 다녀왔다. 화려했
던 콘서트 말미, RM이 진심을 담아 건넨 엔딩 멘트를 돌이
켜본다. "우리의 가사 한 마디라도 여러분이 여러분을 사
랑하는 데 도움이 됐기를 바랍니다."

〈Love Yourself〉 앨범 시리즈를 발표하면서 방탄
소년단은 2년 반 동안 끊임없이 '우리 자신을 사랑하자'
고 말해왔다. '당신이 당신일 수 있도록 자신의 목소리를

event. However, what was more interesting to me was how ARMY, rather than getting angry, tried to understand the phenomenon in a disinterested manner, devising a strategy for how BTS's global fandom should respond to the issue. "White Paper Project".[19]

In this case, fans from all different walks of life gathered from all over the world to discuss the overview of controversy, the historical background of the Japanese invasion of Korea, as well as seeking the particular perspectives of the J-ARMY (ARMY in Japan). An open paper was eventually published describing the entire process, with the results broadcast on the above website. The project did not become very widely known in the end, but it nonetheless created a strong and resounding empathy among BTS fans - an achievement that no Korean governmental body managed to accomplish.

After I came back to Korea, I went to the final ⟨Love Yourself: Speak Yourself⟩ concert in Seoul

내라'고도 이야기해왔다. 우리의 팬덤이 조건 없이 자신들을 지지하기만 하는 일방적인 관계가 아니라 우리도 우리 자신을 찾아가는 동행의 과정으로 삼자고 끊임없이 말을 건네 왔다. 지금도 방탄소년단은 현재 고민하는 것들, 그것을 대하는 태도를 다양한 매체를 통해 아미에게 보여준다. 가끔은 그들이 원하지 않았던 성공을 우리가 계속 요구하는 것이 아닐까, 그들이 우리의 꿈을 대신해서 이루어가는 건 아닐까 하는 '21세기 종교적인 원죄 의식'을 갖게 될 정도로 말이다.

보이밴드 하나를 좋아하게 된 것뿐인데 마치 종합선물세트처럼 안겨온 특별한 경험들 그리고 관계들. 방탄소년단 음악에서 받았던 위로와 기쁨의 시간, 아미들을 통해 확장되는 경험과 세계가 즐겁다.

시작은 방탄소년단이었다. '나 자신을 사랑하는 것이 진정한 사랑의 시작'이라는 방탄소년단의 메시지는 나도 몰랐던, 지금을 살아가는 내게 꼭 필요했던 것이었다. 열심히, 잘 살아야 한다는 프레임에 갇혀 매번 자책했지만 무엇을 위한 자책이었는지 생각하지 않았다. 자주

on October 29th, 2019. At the end of this splendid concert, RM made a sincere remark: "We hope our lyrics have helped you love each other."

Since the 〈Love Yourself〉 album series was released, over the past two-and-a-half years, BTS have been hitting home the message 'Let us love ourselves'. They have also been telling their fans to 'make our own voices so we can be our true selves'. The band did not want an asymmetrical relationship in which their fandom unconditionally supported them; instead they continuously encouraged them to share the journey of finding who we truly were. To date, BTS have been showing ARMY their true thoughts and feelings, through a variety of different media.

After all, while I just happened to fall in love with a single boy band, all the experiences that followed have been truly special. I enjoy so much the consolation and joy that BTS's music has brought, as well as the breadth of experience I have gained through being a part of ARMY.

Everything began with BTS. Their message "Loving yourself is the beginning of a true

찾아오는 우울감은 숨겨야 할 것이었고 쿨한 모습만 보여주려 했다. 하지만 방탄소년단의 앨범과 RM의 믹스테잎 〈mono.〉를 들으며 지금의 나를 솔직히 드러내는 것이 때론 필요하다는 것을 알았다. 그들이 아티스트와 그 이면의 자신을 동시에 보여주었고 팬들이 반응한 것처럼 말이다. 아미라는 복잡다단한 팬덤은 내게 위안과 자극을 동시에 주었다. 나와 다르지 않은 사람이 많다는 것에 위안을 느꼈고, 순수하게 아티스트를 지지하는 모습, 다양한 재능으로 만들어내는 콘텐츠와 프로젝트 그리고 그 속에 담긴 시선들이 나를 자극했다. 물론 팬덤이 커지면서 입덕 초기에는 느끼지 못한 스트레스도 SNS를 통해 흘러들어오곤 한다. 화가 너무 많은 트위터 세상을 가끔은 찢어버리고 싶다고 생각하지만 그럼에도 다시 로그인을 하게 되는 건 실체를 모르지만 분명 실체를 가진 팬덤 아미에 대한 믿음 때문이었다. 방탄소년단과 나, 방탄소년단과 아미, 아미와 나. 어떤 산업도 만들어내지 못할 이 네트워크가 특별하기만 하다. 물론 뉴미디어의 변화도 놓치지 않았다. 2019년엔 빅히트 엔터테인먼트에서

love" was something I so needed in my life, but something I was not aware of. My life was framed by an obsession to live well and live hard, and I had been self-reproaching without knowing what the reproach was for. I often felt depressed, but obliged to hide that feeling and cover it up with being cool. But as I listened to BTS's album as well as RM Mixtape 〈Mono.〉, I came to realise the necessity of opening myself up from time to time. In return, BTS members showed different aspects of their lives - as artists and as candid individuals, and fans reacted gratefully to them.

ARMY, this most sophisticated fandom, gave me both comfort and stimulation. I felt relieved that there were so many people who are not so different from me, and I was motivated by people's genuine desire to support BTS, through various projects and activities grown from their talents, and by a spectrum of perspectives packed into the fandom. Of course, as the fandom grew, some extra sources of stress crept in through SNS, things which I did not see at the beginning of my geeking out. Sometimes, I was going mad, and felt

팬 커뮤니티 '위버스'와 팬 커머스 플랫폼 '위플리'(위버스 샵으로 명칭 변경)를 런칭했다. 평가는 차치하고 이런 사업적인 시도들을 지켜보는 것은 흥미롭다.

누군가 "왜 방탄소년단이 좋아요?"라고 물어오면 이제 나는 이렇게 대답한다. "무엇보다 음악이 좋아서요." 곡 하나하나의 디테일, 그들이 추구해온 음악의 맥락을 자세히 들여다보길 바란다.

나는 오늘도 방탄소년단을 좋아한다. 그러나 그것은 나를 위한 것임을 안다. 그들이 계속 알려주었을 수도 있고 내가 알아챘을 수도 있다. 어찌했던 나는 좋은 사람이 되고 싶다.

as if I wanted to tear myself away from the Twitter world, but then I signed back into social media - with the belief in ARMY, a community that might be constructed but which truly exists. BTS and I, BTS and ARMY, ARMY and I: I cherish this special network that would otherwise never have existed elsewhere.

I love BTS. But also I know that loving BTS is something I do for myself. Perhaps BTS let me realise this, or perhaps I may have come to recognise it on my own. Whatever the case, I hope to remain a carefree and loving person, and to stay loyal to the cause.

삼장.

Chapter Three.

어쩌다 케이팝 산업 한가운데서

—

제인 도

영화 〈나쁜 피〉에서 라디오를 켜기 전, 드니 라방은 말했
다. 틀기만 하면 마음에 맞는 음악이 흘러나온다고. 그처
럼 켜기만 하면 위로가 되는 방송을 하고 싶었다. 멸망으
로 인도하는 문은 크고 넓어 그리로 들어가는 자가 많고
생명으로 인도하는 문은 좁고 협소하여 찾는 이가 적다는
〈좁은 문〉의 구절을 계시처럼 받들어 여러 번 방송사 공채
의 문을 두드렸다.[20] 그러나 합격의 문은 예상했던 것보다
너무 좁았고 여러 번 낙방을 겪자 단단한 줄 알았던 내 멘
탈도 흔들리기 시작했다. 이제 좀 넓은 문을 향해 살아야
되지 않겠나 하는 마음으로 대학원에 진학했고 피디의 꿈

In the midst of the K-pop industry

—

Jane Do

In the film, 〈Bad Blood〉 (1986), Denis Lavant said, just before turning on the radio, "You just turn it on and you get the very tune that was humming inside your head". I wanted to run a broadcast that would be a consolation for the viewers as they turn it on. So I knocked on the door of broadcasters several times, despite a series of failures, taking it as gospel that you enter heaven through a narrow gate, for wide and broad is the gate that leads to destruction and many things can pass through it, but narrow and small is the gate that leads to life even though only few may find it.[20] My gate of acceptance was much narrower than I had anticipated, however, and my lack of success started niggling in my mind. This was why I decided to go to graduate school, to follow a path towards a wider gate, nearly giving up on

도 흐릿해지는 줄 알았다. 석사를 마칠 무렵, 습관처럼 그러나 이번엔 진짜 마지막 시험이라고 생각하고 도전한 방송사 시험에 덜컥 합격했다. 나름 드림스 컴 트루.

어릴 때 TV로만 보던 연예인이 내 앞에 있는 현실이라니 정말로 꿈을 이룬 게 아니냐 혼자 감격할 때도 있다. 애석하지만 그런 순간은 아주 잠깐뿐이다. 과연 내가 꿈꾸고 바라던 피디가 되었느냐에 대해서는 자신이 없기 때문이다. 피디란 종족에게는 원래부터 제작 자율성이 부여된 줄 알았는데 막상 방송국에 들어와 보니 웬걸, 마음대로 할 수 있는 게 거의 없다는 걸 알아버렸다. 게다가 나는 내향적이고 진지한 편이라 예능 피디와 어울리지 않는다는 소리도 듣는다. 그러거나 말거나 피디인 줄 몰랐다는 말보다는 낫다고 생각하고 넘기는 편이다.

웃음 제조, 음주 가무는 서투를지 몰라도 아름다운 것에 열광하고 건강한 재미를 추구한다. 어쩌면 남들이 생각하는 예능 피디 같지 않은 피디인 게 나의 정체성일 것이다. 이 글 역시 음악 방송 프로듀서가 아닌(이 말인즉슨 방탄소년단을 볼 기회가 거의 없다는 의미) 케이팝의 '언저리'에

my dream of becoming a television producer. I continued to apply for this job right until the end of my master's degree, almost monotonously, holding that each time would be my last try. And somehow, on the last attempt, I finally made it. Well, it seems that dreams really do come true.

Occasionally I got emotional, thinking I might have truly achieved my dream, those moments I realise that the celebrities from television were actually stood in front of me. Sadly, such moments were very much short-lived, and I was not entirely sure if I had become the producer my mind had dreamt of. I really thought that the species called producers would have the independence and autonomy to produce programmes as they liked. But the reality was, well, not quite the same. Besides, being more on the introvert and sober side in terms of my personality, I would often hear that I was not really material for the entertainment show bracket. So I just want to elucidate that this essay is based on my personal innermost thoughts as a producer working around the periphery of K-pop rather than as a music broadcast producer:

있는 피디로서 개인의 소회임을 미리 밝혀둔다.

●

방탄소년단이 세계를 휩쓸고 있다. 비틀즈를 잇는 그룹이
라는 찬사에 이어 영국에서는 차기 방탄소년단을 찾겠다
는 목표로 오디션 프로그램까지 생겨날 예정이다. 참으로
글로벌한 인기다. 그런데 나만 홀로 이 인기의 광풍 속에
서 심드렁한 기분이다.

　참고로 나는 한국의 방송사에서 예능 프로그램을 만
들고 있는 예능 피디다. 덕분에 아이돌을 만날 기회는 적
지 않다. 그러나 나는 누굴 봐도 흥분한 적 없는 '평온'한
사람이다. 어차피 일로 만난 사이인데 괜히 환호라도 내
지르면 프로페셔널해 보이지 않을까 봐 마음을 다잡기도
하지만 실제로 누군가의 팬인 적도 없었다.

　"아 진짜 너무 잘생겼어!"

this means, I never got much of a chance to see or work with BTS.

●

BTS also seems to have achieved their dream. They are acclaimed to be the Beatles of our generation. In the UK, an audition programme will soon launch with the objective to find the next BTS. What a global craze this is. But I feel somehow I was left uninterested and alone in the midst of the BTS craze.

For the sake of reference, I am an TV enter-tainment producer, making entertainment shows at one of the Korean broadcasting stations. Thanks to my job, I do get a few chances to meet different K-pop idol singers and groups. But believe or not, I tend to stay unawed, no matter whom it is that I meet. Sometimes, I settle myself down to focus on work, as losing my nerve or cheering may make me look unprofessional in this business relationship anyway. But whatever the case, I have never been a real fan of any band.

"Wow, they are so handsome!" "That is so

"너무 멋있어!"

"내가 아이돌과 함께 일하는 사람이 되다니 성공한 덕후네!"

자신이 좋아하는 아이돌을 만난 동료 피디들 중엔 감탄하는 이들도 적지 않다. 그 순간 그들은 세상에서 가장 신나고 행복한 얼굴로 일을 한다. 가슴속부터 차오르는 그 행복감은 대체 뭐지? 아이돌에게 감흥을 느껴본 적 없는 나로선 이해 못 할 감정이다. 그건 방탄소년단에 대해서도 마찬가지다.

히드로 공항에 있는 세관 아저씨가 "두 유 노 BTS?"라고 물어서 신기하긴 했지만 그렇다고 흥분되지는 않았다. 선배가 두바이에 있는 친구에게 방탄소년단 사인 CD를 보냈건만 중간에 증발돼버렸다는 이야기까지 들었고, "남의 물건을 뜯어 훔쳐갈 만큼의 인기라니, 오 대단하네!" 했지만 정말로 '이게 케이팝의 현 주소라고?' 마냥 고개를 끄덕이기엔 내 안의 심드렁함이 사라지지도 않는다.

물론 예능 피디라면 슈퍼스타의 탄생을 예감하지는

cool!" "I can't believe I am a TV producer working with K-pop idols, I'm such a successful geek!"

Well, quite a few producers and colleagues of mine are excited about meeting and working with their favourite K-pop stars. At such moments, I have seen them working with the happiest and most delighted faces ever. What is that feeling of happiness that rises from deep inside their hearts? As a person who has never been intrigued or inspired by K-pop idols, that is a feeling I would never be able to understand. This is the same, even with BTS.

When I went to the UK in 2018, someone at the border control at Heathrow airport asked me, "Do you know BTS?" This was pretty interesting, but well, not exciting at all. A colleague of mine once told me the story of how the BTS-signed CD she sent over to her friend in Dubai came to disappear in the course of its delivery, and although I then replied sensibly "Wow that's impressive that BTS are so popular that someone even stole it!", that did not quite made my attitude towards K-pop less blasé.

못해도 변화 자체에 민감하게 반응해야 하는 것 아니냐, 반문할 사람도 있을 것이다. 방탄소년단을 통해 콘텐츠를 만들 궁리를 하거나 물들어 올 때 노 젓는다고 케이팝의 해외 진출을 기회로 삼아 기획을 하는 게 능력 있는 프로듀서인 게 아니냐고 말이다.

방탄소년단의 글로벌한 인기는 의심할 여지없이 인정한다. 그러나 이를 무턱대고 좋아하는 게 맞는지는 다른 문제다. 까놓고 말하면 방탄소년단의 성공으로 인해 마치 케이팝 산업 전반이 잘 '운영'되고 있으며 이대로라면 제2의 방탄소년단 탄생도 시간문제라고 여기는 장밋빛 전망은 우려스럽다. 내가 경험한 케이팝, 특히 K-아이돌은 우러러 볼 삶의 형태가 아닌 경우가 많았기 때문이다.

내가 본 K-아이돌은 여자든 남자든 상업적으로 정형화된 틀을 벗어난 경우가 드물었다. 아티스트로서의 매력을 알아차릴 새도 없이 상품으로 소비되는 까닭에 누굴 봐도 비슷해 보였고 조금 덜 여물어서 투박한 느낌이 있었던 가수마저 시장에서 인정하는 상품이 되고자 애쓰는 모습이 안타깝게 느껴졌다. 어쩌면 지금과 같은 방탄

Some might ask, if you are a producer of entertainment shows, then should you not be sensitive to changes in the media industry, even if you might not have forecast the birth of a new rock star? A talented producer should be able to strike while the iron is hot, taking advantage of K-pop's overseas success to make some BTS-related content or plan new programmes accordingly.

I acknowledge that BTS is, undoubtedly, globally popular. But whether I blindly welcome that popularity is a different matter. Let's face it. I am concerned about the all-too-rosy success that the K-pop industry is enjoying, and while it is only a matter of time till the next BTS is found, to me the world of K-pop, and especially the lives of K-singers, is not something to be idolised.

Rarely have the K-idols I have seen, either girls or boys, deviated from a commercially established and standardised formula. Everyone looks as if were created to be consumed as products, and rarely have they had a chance to build their own charm as an artist. A few newcomers to the field with growing talent show some fresh

소년단의 공고한 팬덤은 그들이 대형 기획사 소속이 아니기 때문에 가능했던 걸 수도 있다. 소속사의 간섭이 최소화된 상태에서 트위터, 블로그를 이용해 아직 다듬어지기 이전, '날 것'의 모습을 여과 없이 공개함으로써 팬과의 거리감을 좁혔던 게 효과적이었던 것이다.

부와 명예를 가져다 줄 '공인된 상품성'을 획득하는 방법은 대형 기획사의 노하우로 축적되어 있을지언정 그것이 언제나 성공한다는 보장은 없다. 그러나 K-아이돌에게 바라는 대중의 환상 혹은 아이돌 스스로가 자신을 훈련하는 방식을 보면 세상이 이래도 되나 싶을 만큼 기이한 면이 존재한다.

내가 속한 업계에서는 해외 팬이 케이팝에 흥미를 느끼는 이유를 10대 아티스트가 완성도 높은 무대를 꾸미는 것이 경이롭기 때문이란 분석을 내놓는다. 라이브 보컬리스트

ideas at first, but it is a shame to see that they also soon strive to follow the standardised format to become recognised as a marketable product. Perhaps BTS's current fandom was made possible precisely because they were not part of a large entertainment company. Their agency exerted minimal influence over how they developed their profile, and BTS members revealed their unfiltered side on Twitter and blogs, and this "raw" side of their profile would surely been key in narrowing the distance between them and their fans early on.

Large entertainment agencies in Korea have accumulated extensive knowledge and know-how over the last few decades about how to build K-idols into a kind of merchandise with a "certified commercial value" in order to bring them wealth and fame, even though success is not guaranteed. But having seen the public fantasies surrounding K-idols, and the way those boy bands and girl groups train and discipline themselves, I wonder whether this is the way things should be.

로서 완성도는 일단 제쳐두고라도 '우와' 할 만한 무대를
보여줬다면 이들이 겪었을, 그러나 대중은 알 수 없는 이전
의 시간에 대해 상상해본다. 아마도 그는 미성년자, 어쩌
면 10대 이전부터 '빼어난 외모'로 기획사에 의해 발굴됐을
것이며 일찍부터 철저한 관리를 거쳐 데뷔 무대를 치렀을
것이다.

　기획사에서는 춤과 노래를 잘하는지 조금은 살폈을
테지만 실제로 신인개발팀(A&R, Artist and Repertoire) 관계
자와 얘기를 해보면 "어리고 눈에 띄는 외모일수록" 경쟁
력이 있음을 숨기지 않는다. 아이돌 산업에서 비주얼이
강력한 무기임을 인정하며 이를 적극 장려하는 순간부터
비극은 시작된다.

　"세상이 원래 다 그렇잖아."

　그렇게 넘기기에 이들은 아직 너무 어리다. 자아가
형성되기도 전에 대중이 원한다는 이유로 특정 캐릭터에
자신을 맞춰 가는 훈련을 당연시한다. 그 과정에서 10대

Some experts in my field have analysed how non-Korean fans have become interested in K-pop because they are amazed to see how teenage artists can set up such as elaborate stage shows and deliver such exquisite performances. Leaving aside their competence as live vocalists, however, when they "wow" audiences at their performances, people may picture the time and experiences they must have gone through before they were famous. Probably, they were unearthed when they were still a minor talent by an agency due to his or her good looks, and they must have been trained thoroughly by experts before their debut.

Such agency operators may have checked whether they are also naturally talented at singing and dancing, but among the A&R (Artist and Repertoire) scouts, it is no secret that "the younger and better-looking, the better they are". When one's appearance is acknowledged as the best weapon in the K-pop industry, and its weaponisation is encouraged, that's where the tragedy surely begins.

소녀들의 다이어트는 성공을 위한 필수 과정처럼 인식된다. 닭가슴살 60g를 다섯 번 나눠먹는 것은 기본. 탄수화물을 최소화하고 단백질 위주의 식단과 운동을 병행하는 '걸 그룹 다이어트'는 "깜짝 컴백! 누구누구 몇 kg 감량"과 같은 헤드라인으로 화제가 된다.

성장기 소녀들은 화장실에서 몰래 과자를 먹으며 허기를 달래지만 아이돌이 되려면 마땅히 예쁘고 날씬해야 하므로 그저 견디는 게 일이다. 연습생 기간 동안 목표 몸무게를 초과하면 바로 OUT! 꿈을 이룰 기회가 박탈되기 때문이다. 그런데 이들이 화려한 스포트라이트를 받으며 케이팝의 대표주자로 성공하면, 학대에 가까운 이 모든 과정은 괜찮은 게 되는 걸까? 이것은 엔터테인먼트 산업의 종사자인 나에게 묻는 질문이기도 하다. 나는 아이돌을 대중에게 보여주는 사람으로서 어떻게 재현하고 묘사할지, 충분히 성찰하고 있는 것일까?

아이돌을 재현하는 방식에는 일종의 스테레오 타입이 존재한다. 일단 여자 아이돌은 밝고 명랑하고 청순하되 예의도 바르고 잘 웃어야 한다. 아니 정확히 말하자

"Well, that's just how the world is."

But these kids are yet too young for their problems to be brushed off like that. They take as natural the training to refashion themselves towards a specific image, even before they have become mature, just because this is what the public want. Over the course of this process, the teenage girls going on a diet is an essential part of the roadmap to success. Eating 60g of chicken breast five meals a day is a basic factor. Minimal intake of carbs combined with protein-focused diet and exercise is now called the "girl group diet". Phrases like "Surprise comeback! XXX has lost YYY pounds" often appear as entertainment news headlines.

Girls in their adolescence appease their hunger eating sweets in secret in bathrooms, but this is something they need to endure as they must remain pretty and slim to become an idol singer. If you happen to exceed the target weight while in training, that means you are OUT! Your opportunity to achieve the dream of being a star is gone for good. But if one eventually comes

면, 여자 아이돌에게 세상이 기대하는 그림이 그러한 것
이라고들 믿는다.

　　남자 아이돌 그룹 매니저는 입담이 좋은 사람, 캐릭
터가 독특한 사람 등 멤버의 특징을 어필하며 섭외 요청
을 하지만 여자 그룹의 경우에는 '비주얼 멤버' 위주로 홍
보를 한다. 심지어 연습생 커리큘럼도 남자 아이돌은 작
곡법과 같은 프로듀싱 과정이나 실력 향상 위주로 짜여
있지만 여자 아이돌은 그렇지 않다고 한다. 이미 기획 단
계부터 다르게 취급받는 것에 약간의 충격을 받았음을
고백한다.

to succeed as a K-idols and win the glory of the spotlight, then does this justify such processes that are almost akin to abuse? This is also the question that I ask myself, working in the entertainment industry. Do I offer enough reflection on how I represent and describe idol singers and groups?

There are certain stereotypes of how K-idols are to be represented. For instance, girl groups should be bright, cheerful and innocent, but also polite and smiley. More precisely, I believe this is what the world expects from them.

Managers of boy bands often promote members' characteristics, such as this guy is a good talker or nicely idiosyncratic, when liaising with the broadcast staff; while girl group managers generally market more the so-called "visual members", the good-looking ones. Even the training curriculums for boy bands and girl groups are different. The former tends to teach composing skills and producing, with more overall focus on improving their musical competence, but this is not the case for girl groups. I must confess I was shocked when I first learnt they are treated so

differently from the start.

The production staff are also responsible for this situation. Every time a girl group arrives on a show, they ask for "Aegyo", a cute (sometimes coquettish) display of affection often expressed through a cute voice, facial expression or gesture, as if that is the way they should be. If a girl group member is perplexed and refused to show "Aegyo", then it is almost commonplace that their behaviour becomes the hot topic in the next day's entertainment news. Recently, some girl group members were heavily criticised by some male fans for carrying a mobile phone case with the phrase "Girls can do anything", and reading "Kim Ji-young: Born 1982" (a feminist book in Korea).[21]

Some fans who seemingly want to see the girls just as pretty and vivacious may be so dismayed that they will renounce their fandom. Do they really want smiling dolls with no ego, thought or self-reflexivity? I pray for the peace of mind of Korean girl groups. To the eyes of me, a third-party spectator, there is a whole lot of ridiculous nonsense involved, and I wonder if these teenage

　　방송 제작진의 책임도 피할 수 없는 게 여자 아이돌만 출연하면 정해진 수순처럼 애교를 보여 달라 난리다. 애교 요청에 난감해하며 거부하면 다음 날 '태도 논란'으로 연예면 기사를 장식하는 건 너무나 익숙한 클리셰다. 최근에는 여성 아이돌이 'Girls can do anything'이 새겨진 휴대전화 케이스를 들고 다녀서, 또는 〈82년생 김지영〉을 읽었다는 이유로 남성 팬들의 광분을 샀다.[21] 예쁘고 밝고 청량한 이미지로만 소비하겠다는 마음에 상처를 받은 이들은 당당하게 팬 철회 선언까지 한다. 자아도 생각도 없고 판단도 하지 않을, 방긋 웃어주는 인형을 바라는 심보라니, 한국의 여성 아이돌의 멘탈은 과연 괜찮은 걸까? 지켜보는 내 입장에서도 말도 안 되는 일들의 연속인데 말이다.

한국을 대표하는 아트 디렉터 중 한 명인 박찬욱 감독의

girl groups have a strong enough mindset to handle it all. Do they have the right mental foundation?

●

In the film ⟨Handmaiden⟩, directed by Park, Chan-wook, one of the Korea's leading "auteur" directors, there is a scene in which Lady Hideko reads erotic novels in front of several men (all full of voyeuristic desire). A colleague of mine who watched the movie once disclosed that she felt shocked when it occurred to her that she might be like those hordes of men, sexually charged and objectifying Hideko. This introspection led her to the further realisation that she might have actively aided and abetted the representation of girl groups as bright, cheerful and cute, dismissing any concerns with the thought, 'That's what public want so I can represent them as such'. She has my deepest sympathies there.

Perhaps, I have mistaken what I do as something which is "good for all". Appearing on TV is a crucial opportunity for any K-idol who has undergone years of training, and a television

영화 〈아가씨〉 중에는 히데코(김민희)가 관음증적 욕망으로 득실거리는 남자들 앞에서 에로틱한 텍스트를 읽는 장면이 나온다. 영화를 본 내 동료는 히데코를 전시하고 대상화하는 남자들 무리에 자신도 속한 게 아닌가 섬뜩했다고 고백한 적이 있다. 밝고 잘 웃고 상큼한 여성 아이돌만 살아남는 세상이니까, 대중의 욕망이 원래 그런 거니까 관성적으로 담아내면 되지, 어쩌면 자신도 방조해왔던 게 아닐까, 하는 반성. 나 역시 깊이 공감했다.

그동안은 내가 하는 일이 '모두에게 좋은' 거라고 착각했던 것 같다. 수 년 간의 연습생 시절을 겪은 아이돌에게 방송 출연은 자신을 내비칠 매우 중요한 기회고, 피디는 그런 기회를 주는 사람이니까. 피디로서 나는 좋은 일을 한 게 아닐까? 그렇게 믿고 싶었는지도 모른다. 관행적이고 무비판적인 방식으로 성적 대상화에 일조했을지도 모르는데, 그래서 출연자의 내면에 생채기를 냈을지도 모르는데 지나치게 무심하게 그들의 삶을 함부로 단정 지었다.

변명을 하자면 제작자로서 현장에서 느끼는 고정관

producer is someone who offers such an opportunity. So, as a producer, I have probably done something good, right? Perhaps that is what I wanted to believe - though in reality, I may have aided sexual objectification or hurt someone's feelings in a thoughtless and uncritical manner. Might I not have judged them too quickly with my indifference?

Indeed, and in my slight defence, the wall of stereotypes I find on site as a producer is stronger and taller than you would expect. Many broadcasting staff still hold the view that "women should be young and pretty". If you try to liaise and approach girl groups from somewhat different angles, then production crews express complaints and make a stink about why they should take a risk, or what happens if the ratings fall.

I bet things are more flexible for boy bands. For instance, if they are offhand and unsociable, they are seen as chicly reticent. If they are not good-looking but are good talkers, they are born for entertainment. Under any circumstance. They will be ascribed unique characteristics. I am very

념의 벽은 예상보다 높고 견고하다. 특히나 여성 출연자
에 대한 방송 관계자의 인식은 "여자는 젊고 예뻐야 한
다" 수준에서 크게 나아지지 않아서 회의감이 들 때가 있
다. 조금 다른 시각으로 섭외를 시도하려고 하면 제작진
들 사이에서도 이미 불만이 터진다. 굳이 왜 모험을 감수
하려 드냐고, 시청률 떨어지면 어떡하냐고 난리다. 단언
컨대 남자 아이돌에게는 훨씬 관대하다. 무뚝뚝하면 시
크남, 재미가 없으면 노잼돌, 잘생기지 않더라도 입담이
좋으면 예능돌, 어떤 상황에서든 캐릭터가 형성된다. 가
끔은 너무 궁금하기도 하다. 외모로 대놓고 차별받는 여
자 아이돌과 다르게 무엇을 해도 지지받고 응원 받는 기
분이란 대체 뭘까? 나는 영원히 모를 것 같다.

방탄소년단과 만난 적이 있다. 방탄소년단은 지금이야 슈
퍼스타지만 2015년 5월만 해도 KBS 〈안녕하세요〉 예

curious about this. Unlike girl groups who are discriminated against for their looks, how would they feel if they were supported and cheered no matter what? Perhaps we will never know.

❦

I once had a chance to meet BTS. Now they are superstars, but in May 2015, they were rookies who could not hide their anxiety before their first appearance on KBS's talk show 〈Hello Counselor〉. Fresh-faced and pristine, somewhat different from boy bands and girl groups from large entertainment agencies - this was my first impression of BTS. One of their company officials said that the newly released album was made with money out of their own pockets, and added "If this doesn't work, we are in trouble".

I felt bad for them, and felt eager for their success. A long time later, after they had almost slipped from my mind - Bammmmmmm! They became total celebrities. Whew! I'm saying it now because they are successful, but isn't it too risky a business that the company staff had to invest their

능 첫 출연을 앞두고 긴장한 티를 못 숨기는 신인 그룹이
었고 어찌 보면 결연해보이기까지 했다. 대형 기획사의 아
이돌과는 다른 어딘가 풋풋한 이미지, 그게 나의 첫 인상
이었다. 관계자는 사비를 털어서 투자한 음반이기 때문에
"이번에 잘되지 않으면 모두가 위험하다"고 덧붙이기도 했
다. 괜히 짠한 마음도 들면서 잘되길 바랐는데 이후 모든
걸 잊을 때 즈음 Bammmmmmm! 슈퍼스타가 되었다.
어휴, 이제 와 하는 말이지만 잘됐으니 망정이지 솔직히 개
인 재산까지 다 투자할 정도면 너무 위험한 산업이 아닌
가. 누가 언제 대박을 터뜨릴지 알 수 없지만 올~인, 베팅
을 거는 도박이라니 이게 정상적인 방식은 아니어야 맞지
않나.

자신들의 미래가 위험할 수도 있다는 걸 아는지 모
르는지 신인이었던 방탄소년의 뷔와 RM은 해맑았다. 출
연자의 고민을 열심히 경청하던 RM은 노력은 하지 않으
면서 꿈만 꾸는 사람에게 자신이 가수가 되기 위해 부모
님을 설득했던 경험담을 털어 놓았다. 공부를 꽤나 잘했
던 그가 갑자기 가수가 된다고 하니까 부모님의 반대가

own money? You never know who will hit the jackpot, or when, yet had to bet all in this gamble; this could not be a normal way of doing business.

I wonder if they knew their futures were hanging on a cliff-edge during that first show. V and RM's faces were bright. RM, who was carefully listening to the concerns of the daydreaming audience on the show, shared his own experience of how he convinced his parents to let him pursue music. His parents were shocked at his dream to become a singer, and were heavily opposed to it, especially because RM was a gifted student. But he persuaded them by making his aspiration clear: "I am the number one student in my school, but I will be the number one rapper in the world too". Heart-warming and touching as this story was, it did not appear on the final broadcast due to a lack of laughter and fun in it. Time constraints snipped off much of his story. Furthermore, in V's case, only brief comments of his like "I'm worried" and "I'm not worried" made the airwaves. Their debut was challenging in a world of entertainment where you should amuse, or fade away. But this may

무척 심했지만 "시험을 보면 전교생 중에 1등이지만 랩으로는 전 세계 1등을 할 것"이라며 당당한 포부를 밝혀 부모님의 마음을 돌렸다는 아주 훈훈한 이야기다. 감동은 있었지만 웃음과 재미가 부족했던 RM의 말은 방송에서는 찾아보기 힘들다. 시간 관계상 싹둑! 대부분 잘려나갔기 때문이다. 심지어 뷔는 "고민이에요", "고민이 아니에요" 정도로 단답형 대답만 전파를 탔다. 웃음을 유발하지 않으면 버려지는 예능의 세계에서 그들의 데뷔는 만만치 않았다. 그렇지만 이 정도 일화는 슈퍼스타가 신인이었을 때 겪을 법한 재미있는 이야깃거리 정도는 될 것 같다.

　　그러고 보니 팬들에게 재미없게 들릴 이야기도 하나 있다. 2016년 즈음 나는 방탄소년단의 팬과 메신저로 엄청나게 싸우게 된다. 사건의 발단은 이랬다. 상대는 방탄소년단의 광팬이자 옛 동료였고 우리는 안부를 주고받으며 반가운 인사를 나눴다. 그러다 자신의 조카가 페미니즘에 관심이 많다는 이야기가 나왔고, 방탄소년단도 페미니즘 공부를 하는지 책장에 어떤 책이 있더라 하고 내게 말을 건넸다. 그런데 나는 논란이 됐던 방탄소년단

have been a fun thing to note for these superstars at the beginning of their careers.

Come to think of it, I have another BTS-related story, albeit one that may not interest BTS fans. Around 2016, I got involved in a huge quarrel with a BTS fan in an online chat. Here is how that began. She was an old colleague of mine and a BTS fanatic, and we said hello and exchanged pleasantries and idle chatter. Then she said her niece had become interested in feminism and added that BTS also had some books about feminism on their shelf so they would probably have been studying it, too. Unfortunately that reminded me of the then-controversial lyrics of the song, and how I found them unpleasant, so I bombarded her with barbed comments about BTS, like 'It's obvious how they see women, but they wouldn't even know if they did anything wrong, they are so popular their fans would die to cover up their faults'. In hindsight, she probably just brought up that whole story as a topic geared to appeal to my long-standing interest in feminism. But my sarcastic response would not have made her very

의 노래 가사가 너무 불쾌한 나머지 원래 여자에 대한 생각이 어떤지 너무 잘 알겠다, 하지만 인기가 많다는 이유로 팬들이 감싸주니 본인 잘못이 뭔지도 모를 거다 등등 내 생각을 쏟아냈다. 상대는 페미니즘에 관심 많은 내게 '맞춘' 화제였는데 반응이 삐딱하니 기분 좋을 리 없었고 냉랭한 대화가 오고갔다.

나와 말다툼을 벌였던 친구는 방탄소년단은 여타 아이돌 그룹 음악과 완성도 면에서 다르다며 직접 들어보라고 했지만 여성 비하적인 가사와 발언을 포용할 만한 재능과 매력이란 건 세상에 존재하지 않는다는 게 내 생각이었다. 어떤 면에서 아이돌에 대한 나의 무심함은 잘못을 해도 무조건적으로 이해받고 용서받는 남자 아이돌에 대한 냉소인 것이기도 했다.

그렇다고 내가 방탄소년단의 세계적 인기와 그들이 거둔 성과를 폄하하려고 이 글을 쓰는 것은 아니다. 이후 방탄소년단과 빅히트 엔터테인먼트는 변화된 모습을 보여주었기 때문이다. 문화 트렌드를 만들어 나가는 아이돌 그룹의 일원으로서 사회에 큰 영향을 미칠 수 있음

happy, and killed the mood of our conversation.

She argued that BTS's songs are different from those of other K-idol groups, in terms of their musical excellence if nothing else, and insisted I listen to their music. But in my honest opinion, sexist lyrics and remarks cannot be tolerated in any area, no matter how talented and charming its proponents are. To some extent, my indifference to K-idols comes from my cynicism towards boy bands, whose mistakes are more generously understood and forgiven.

Let me be clear, however, I am not writing this to disparage or belittle the global popularity and achievement of BTS. They and their agency Big Hit Entertainment have shown how they have changed. They announced clearly that the recognition of their potentially profound influence over society as K-idols at the forefront of cultural trends, has made them act and behave more sensitively. Perhaps the books on feminism found on RM's bookshelf were in part testifying to this resolution. Also, I have to admit that the BTS live performance singing and dancing at the 2017 KBS

을 인지하고 신중하겠다고 입장을 밝혔다. 2017년 KBS 〈가요대축제〉에서 방탄소년단은 올 라이브 밴드로 춤과 노래를 소화했는데 나로서도 감탄할 수밖에 없는 무대였음을 솔직히 밝힌다.

그러니까 이 글의 '진짜' 목적은 방탄소년단을 비롯한 수많은 아이돌의 가치가 상품성과 직결되는 케이팝 산업에서 미성년 연습생에 대한 지원과 보호가 공개적으로 논의되어야 한다는 주장을 하기 위함이다.

내가 목도한 여성/남성 아이돌의 '차이'는 기획 및 훈련 과정에서부터 시작된 것이다. 미성년자일 때부터 아이돌로 훈련된 이들은 최소한의 학업 기회도 주어지지 않았기 때문에 성인지 감수성 교육도 제대로 이뤄질 리가 없다. 혹시나 겪을지 모를 악플이나 헤이트 스피치로 정신적 충격을 받게 될 수도 있다고 경고한 어른은 내가

Song Festival was quite something, even to me.

●

So, the "real" purpose of this essay is to argue that, in the K-pop industry, where BTS, among many other boy bands and girl groups' merits are connected directly with their commercial value and profitability, we need more open discussion on the support and protection of the young would-be K-idol trainees.

The "difference" between boy bands and girl groups in K-pop, as I have witnessed, stems from their management and training procedures. As they are trained to become K-idols from near-infancy, they receive minimal education opportunities and thus few chances to learn about gender sensitivity. To the best of my knowledge, no single adult (in this industry) has warned them about the trauma or mental shock they might come to experience from trolling comments or hate speech. Rather, they say "The one who wants to wear the crown, must bear its weight", more often considering such malicious activities the natural price for stardom.

알기론 없다. 오히려 악플을 '왕관을 쓰려는 자 그 무게를 견디라'며 스타덤이 주는 당연한 대가처럼 여기는 경우는 빈번하다.

이 글을 쓰는 동안 방송가에서 몇 번 봤던 여성 아이돌 출신 가수 두 명이 자살했다. 아이돌에 무심한 나도 감탄할 만큼 무척이나 예쁘고 반짝반짝 빛나던 존재들이었다. 가슴이 너무 아파서 차마 이름을 언급하지 못하겠다. 그 중 한 명은 "내가 어리다는 걸 사람들이 모르는 것 같아요"라고 말한 적이 있다. 스타라는 이유로 모든 비방을 견딜 수 있는 어른도 없을 텐데 그는 너무 어릴 때부터 산업의 한복판에서 정신적 어려움을 토로해왔다. 제발 자신의 아픔을 알아달라고 신호를 보냈지만 알아서 버텨주기를 바라는 동안 케이팝 산업의 내부는 병들어가고 있었다. 매번 재능 있는 아티스트들의 죽음을 접할 때마다 제기된 문제였지만 도약하는 K-wave에 걸림돌이 된다며 제대로 논의된 적이 없기도 했다.

진심으로, 묻고 싶다. 우리가 바라는 K-wave란 대체 어떤 것이냐고? 바라건대, 제발 지금이라도 이들의

While I was writing this essay, two female idol-turned-singers I have met a few times, committed suicide. They were so adorable and bright that even I, someone typically indifferent to K-idols, was impressed. Mentioning their names would be too painful for me and would break my heart. One of them told me that "I don't think people know I'm so young". No adult would be able to withstand the criticisms of being a celebrity, and she had been pouring forth her agony in the K-pop industry since youth. She had also been sending signals about how fraught she was, hoping someone would notice her suffering while trying to take care of things on her own. But the pathologies of K-pop industry were deepening. This is an issue that has repeatedly been raised every time a talented artist dies, but also one that has never been properly addressed, as it may have put up barriers to the rising "Korean Wave".

I therefore raise these questions and concerns with the utmost seriousness. What kind of Korean Wave are we really aspiring to create? I dare argue that the industry must now transform and make

충격적인 죽음이 잊히지 않도록 변해야 할 것이다. 미성
년 연습생의 성인지 감수성 교육, 최소한의 학업 및 안전
망 보장은 이제라도 제대로 이루어져야 한다.

　호황을 누리고 있는 것처럼 보이는 케이팝 산업은
수많은 아이돌의 희생으로 유지돼 왔다. 기획 상품으로
간택 받고 훈련 받아 무대에 서고 팬들의 지갑이 열리면
이들은 비로소 스타가 된다. 잘 나가는 스타가 된다 해도
방심은 금물이다. 이후부터는 인기를 얼마나 더 지속하
느냐가 관건이다. 혹여 상품성이 떨어질 수도 있으니 마
음대로 연애조차 못한다. 대중이 열광할 만한 완벽한 무
대 뒤에 이들이 느낄 허망함을 나는 간접적으로 경험하
곤 한다. 조금이라도 실수하면 오늘의 환호성이 야유가
될 것이라는 두려움에 미래의 생계를 벌써부터 걱정하거
나 팬에게는 무조건 다정하고 친절해야 된다는 이유로
모욕까지 견디는 것도 보았다. 어릴 때부터 기획사의 관
리 체계에 익숙하기 때문에 성인이 되어 제2의 인생을 시
작하려고 해도 세상 물정을 몰라 사기를 당한 경우도 많
다. 무대 밖 아이돌의 일상은 생각보다 빛나지 않았다.

sure the dreadful deaths of these singers will not be forgotten. It is imperative that we teach gender sensitivity to minors and ensure their rights to basic schooling and protection.

The K-pop business seems to be booming. But it is founded and promulgated upon the sacrifices of numerous children who aspire to be idol singers. They become stars once they are chosen as commodities, trained to be on stage, enticing their fans to open their wallets. But even if they managed to become celebrities, they cannot take things easy. The issue at stake for them is then how long they can sustain their success. They do not have the freedom to be in a relationship or even date people, as this might be detrimental to their value as commodities. The public rave about their perfect stage performances, but I have indirectly experienced the feeling of void in their minds. Many of them are already worried about making a future living, out of fear that their tiny mistakes may turn today's cheers to jeers, and they bear strings of insults because they feel they must be friendly and pleasing to their fans. Some, who

이런 생각을 하다 보면 나는 심드렁해질 수밖에 없다. 일터에서 마주치는 반짝반짝 빛나는 스타들과 인사를 해도, 촬영을 해도 나는 크게 동요하지 않는다. 이들의 삶을 조금이라도 들여다보면 이면에 숨겨진 비정한 현실과 아픔을 그냥 지나치기가 힘들다. 그래서 차라리 아무렇지 않은 척 무심한 편을 택한다.

드라마 〈프로듀사〉를 보면 예능 피디가 아이돌 밴드 멤버를 도와주려다 아무 것도 할 수 없는 자신의 처지를 깨닫는 장면이 나온다.[22] 내가 실제로 그런 일을 겪은 적은 없다. 앞으로도 없을 듯하다. 나는 출연자에게 사적인 대화를 건넬 정도로 오지랖이 넓지도 않고 사교성이 뛰어난 피디도 아니니까. 하지만 언제까지 내가 이럴 수 있을지는 모르겠다. 방탄소년단의 성공담을 들으며, 때때로 누군가의 자살 소식을 들으며, 이런 나마저 동요되는 순간이 점점 많아지고 있는 게 문제다.

have started new lives outside the K-pop industry, have become victims of scams and frauds, as they were so used to living under the rock of protection of the entertainment companies. The lives of K-idols off the stage was certainly not as dazzling as I had thought.

Thinking about all this, it is no surprise that I have come to feel blasé about K-pop. Running into, meeting, and even working with starry celebrities have scarcely offered me any emotional highs. When you get to know more of their lives, you can no longer just pass over the cold, hard reality and the suffering hidden behind the dazzling fronts. So, I prefer to feign indifference.

In the Korean drama ⟨The Producers⟩, there is a scene in which an entertainment show produ-cer comes to realise he is not quite in a position to help members of idol groups.[22] I have not been in the same situation, and I am unlikely to experience it, as I am neither nosy nor sociable enough to have private conversations with those who are on the shows. But I am not sure for how long I can maintain this attitude. Listening to the BTS success

케이팝 산업이 전반적으로 바뀌기 전에 내가 할 수 있는 것들에 대해 가끔은 진지하게 생각해 본다. 연예인 '친화적'이지 않은 내가 난데없이 "요즘 많이 힘들지?" 하고 고민 상담사처럼 나서는 건 안 하느니만 못할 터.

2019년 12월 EBS의 〈보니하니〉는 미성년 진행자를 대하는 어른들의 폭력적 태도 때문에 제작이 중단됐다. 사장이 나서서 사과했지만 사건의 장본인인 어른 진행자는 되려 억울해하는 눈치다. 일련의 사건을 겪고도 여전히 속 터지는 일들이 터지다니, 참으로 답답하던 와중에 어린이 배우들과 작업한 윤가은 감독의 기사를 발견했다.[23] 정답은 가까이에 있었다. 윤가은 감독이 고심해서 직접 작성한 촬영 수칙을 요약하면 다음과 같다.

> 어린이 배우를 인격적 주체로 대할 것. 머리를 쓰다듬는 행위 및 신체적 접촉은 사전에 동의를 구할 것. 어린이 배우들 앞에서 언어 사용에 주의할 것, 특히 자존감에 영향을 미칠 수 있는 외적인 부분에 대한 칭찬이나

story, while other girl group members commit suicide, I feel more and more disturbed.

❧

Sometimes, I seriously ponder what I can do to make a difference - to effect the transformation of the K-pop industry into something humane. But I am not the most sociable person, so perhaps it is better for me not to act like a counsellor or try to offer personal solace or comfort.

Not long ago, one of the Korean public broadcasters of the EBS children's show ⟨Tok! Tok! Boni, Hani⟩ was suspended, due to adult hosts' violent attitudes towards the show's teenage hosts. EBS's president apologised publicly, but the "adult host" at the centre of the controversy seemed to grudge the public criticism. It was frustrating to see these kinds of happenings after all the tragedies. Then, I came across an article by director Yoon Ga-eun, who has worked with many child actors and actresses.[23] The way to remedy this situation was not far away from us. What follows is the director's summary of the basic rules to comply with when

품평은 삼가되 배우로서의 태도를 칭찬해줄 것. 무엇
보다 현장에 있는 스태프 개개인은 어린이 배우의 모범
이 되도록 노력할 것.

2018년부터 내가 근무하는 방송국에서 녹화 현장
에 있는 모든 스태프는 성희롱 예방 수칙을 공유하고 지
키려 노력해왔다. 개인적으로는 이것만으로는 충분하
지 않다고 생각한다. 덧붙여 미성년 출연자의 인권을 보
호하는 수칙을 추가하고 촬영 현장뿐 아니라 섭외 단계
부터 편집, 방송에 나가는 과정 내내 지키려고 노력한다
면? 케이팝 산업 전반이 변하기를 넋 놓고 기다리는 것
보다 훨씬 생산적인 일이다. 물론 이조차도 법으로 지정
돼 모든 제작 현장에서 필수적으로 지켜야 할 규범이 된
다면 이상적일 것이다.

예능 피디로서 나는 미성년 아이돌의 카운슬러는
못 돼도 그들이 겪지 말아야 아픔을 예방할 책임이 있다
고 생각한다. 이제부터 앞서 언급한 수칙을 잘 지켜서 시
청자의 공감을 사는 프로그램을 만들어 볼 생각이다. 이

working with children:

> Respect the personal identity of a child actor/
> actress. Any physical contact such as patting
> their head must be agreed in advance. Be
> cautious with use of language in front of child
> actors/actresses. Especially, refrain from judging
> or praising their appearance in ways that might
> have an effect on their self-esteem, and instead
> complement their attitude as an actor/actress.
> Above all, all staff members at the scene should
> try to set good examples for child actors/
> actresses.

Since last year, every staff at the filming site of
the broadcasting station I work for have strived to
share and conform to the rules that help prevent
sexual harassment. In my honest opinion, however,
this is not enough. What if we "also" comply with
the above rules, not just at the site of filming but
also throughout the entire process of production,
from casting to editing and broadcasting? I believe
this may be far more productive than just waiting

러한 나의 다짐은 방탄소년단의 신드롬을 돌아보며 시
작된 것이지만 내가 방탄소년단을 또 만날 날이 과연 올
까? 아마도 그럴 날은 없을 것 같다. 방탄소년단은 너~
무 슈퍼스타여서 살인적인 스케줄을 소화하느라 바쁘기
도 하거니와 예능 피디라고 해서 연예인을 일대일로 마
주할 일이 많은 것은 아니기 때문이다(주로 매니저와 소통한
다). 이럴 줄 알았으면 2015년에 말 좀 걸어볼 걸 그랬다.
평생 한 번, 어쩌면 마지막이었을지도 모르는데 이제와
아쉬운 마음이 들기도 한다.

for the entire K-pop industry to change by itself. Even more preferably, these rules could be turned into laws for every production site to abide by.

I cannot be a counsellor or psychiatrist for K-idols, but as an entertainment producer, I believe I bear the responsibility for preventing suffering that is undeserved. I try to create programmes that "well observe" the above rules and at the same time win the audience's sympathy. This intention all started with my reflection on the BTS phenomenon. Will I ever get to meet the band again? Probably not. BTS are such superstars now that they will not be able to spare time off from their gruelling schedule, and being an entertainment programme producer does not necessarily mean I get many chances to meet celebrities one-on-one. Had I known this, I might have talked more to them in 2015. That may have been a once-in-a-lifetime opportunity, perhaps my last ever, and that is kind of a bummer.

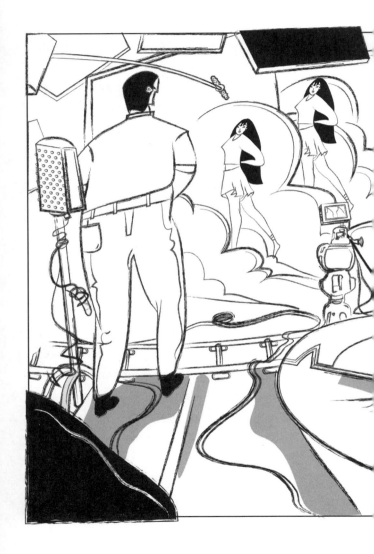

사장.

Chapter Four.

우리 함께, 방탄소년단과 크리스마스

—

지 킴 · 믹 신 · 제인 도

이 책은 지 킴, 믹 신, 제인 도, 이렇게 세 사람이 썼다. 성격은 제각각인데 석사 시절에 문화연구를 공부한 공통점이 있어서인지 정치나 문화 이야기를 할 때는 죽이 잘 맞는다. 지 킴이 방탄소년단에 대한 책을 만들어보자고 처음 제안했을 때는 이견이 갈렸다. 출판기획자인 믹 신은 흔쾌히 하겠노라 했지만 제인 도는 방탄소년단 팬이 아닌 자기가 껴도 되겠냐며 망설였다. 하지만 막상 글은 제일 열심히 썼다. 유일하게 방탄소년단과 직접 만나 일까지 같이 했고 이 책에서는 그 경험에 대해 풀어냈다.

지 킴은 이전부터 아무래도 케이팝에 대한 책을 만

Together, Christmas with BTS

—

Ji Kim · Mick Shin · Jane Do

This book was written by three authors: Ji Kim, Mick Shin, and Jane Do. They have different personalities, but still hit it off when discussing politics or culture, perhaps because they all read cultural studies for their master's degrees. They could not agree on the publication of a book purely on the subject of BTS, however, as when Ji first proposed the idea, Mick Shin (a professional book editor) was keen to proceed, but Jane Do (a non-BTS fan) was reluctant. In the end, it turned out that Jane wrote the most passionately and the most seriously on the subject. Moreover, she was the only one of the three to have actually met BTS in person, or worked with them. Her essay in this book therefore details her valuable experiences working in the K-pop industry.

Ji Kim used to tell her friends that she should

들어야겠다고 두 친구에게 말하곤 했다. 유학을 간 런던에서 8년째 살고 있는데 자꾸만 거리에서 케이팝이 들리고 사람들이 한국어로 말을 걸어오는데 이런 경험들을 학술논문으로 쓸 순 없으니 어쩌야 해, 아무래도 뭐가 됐든 기록으로 남겨야겠다는 것이었다. 방탄소년단을 좋아하게 된 후부터는 자신도 케이팝과 방탄소년단 이야기를 입에 달고 살아 쓸 말이 많았다. 그러다 보니 셋 중 가장 두서없이 글을 썼다.

믹 신은 석사 시절에는 도시공간 연구를 했고 야구 보기를 좋아했다. 방탄소년단을 좋아하게 된 지는 꽤 됐는데 그렇다고 두 친구를 만날 때 방탄소년단 이야기를 구구절절 늘어놓지는 않는다. 나이가 제일 어리고 기가 약해 어떤 화제가 나오든 언니들 말을 얌전하게 들어주는 편이다. 하지만 행동력은 제일 강하고 한 번 시작한 일은 반드시 끝을 맺는다. 스스로 방탄소년단의 덕후라 밝히는 것은 저자 중 그뿐으로 방탄소년단 콘서트를 보러 런던까지 다녀왔다.

이렇게나 다른 세 사람이 방탄소년단에 대한 책을

one day write a book on K-pop. Having lived in London for the last 8 years, ever since she came to the city for study, she has repeatedly heard K-pop on the street and sometimes even met people who speak to her in Korean. It would be difficult to write about these experiences in an academic article, but in whatever format, she was eager to put down a record of them. Since she became a BTS fan herself, she has been chattering about K-pop and BTS non-stop, and has a great deal to write about. Perhaps for this reason, she was sometimes found guilty of rambling in her essay.

Mick Shin, for her part, studied Urban Spaces for her master's, and likes watching baseball. She has been a BTS fan for a while, but that does not necessarily mean she natters on about BTS every time she meets Ji and Jane. As the youngest in the group, and the most quiet and modest, she tends to listen to what the other two have to say, regardless of the topic. But she remains among the most driven of the trio, and is someone who will always get the job done. She is the only author in this book who self-identify as a real BTS geek, and

함께 썼다. 역시나 너무 다른 스타일로 써 각 장마다 필체와 구성 방식이 다르다. 여기까지 읽은 독자가 제일 잘 알 문제다. 독립출판이잖아, 아무래도 괜찮으니 본인이 하고 싶은 이야기만 해, 지 킴이 우겨서 각자 알아서 썼더니 이렇게 돼버렸다. 혹 환불을 받고 싶다면 그녀에게(만) 연락해야 한다.

　이 마지막 장은 아무래도 자기 이야기만 늘어놓고 끝낼 순 없으니 셋이 의견을 모아 끝을 맺어보자 싶어 기획했다. 2019년 12월 25일, 한국 시간으로 저녁 8시부터 2시간 동안 카카오톡의 보이스톡으로 나눈 이야기를 지 킴이 정리했다. 주제는 크게 세 가지, 어쩌다 우리는 케이팝과 방탄소년단을 이야기하게 됐나, 우리에게 방탄소년단은 무엇인가, 이 와중에도 제인 도는 왜 여전히 케이팝이나 방탄소년단에 심드렁한지에 대해서다. 여전히 팬들은 관심 없을 굉장히 사적인 주제들만 이야기해버렸다. 그래도 괜찮다면 마지막까지 읽어주시길.

once flew from Seoul to London just to attend a BTS concert.

These three together wrote a book about K-pop in December, the last month of 2019. Given their idiosyncrasies, their styles of writing and structuring varied considerably from one another. The readers, having read this far, will be well aware of this fact. Ji Kim is partly responsible for this, as she insisted "It's an independent publishing, don't worry [about the format and structure of writing] and write whatever stories you want to tell". This is the book that resulted. So if you would like to request a refund, please contact Ji (not one of the others).

This last chapter is planned in a way to "collectively" wrap up the previous chapters, which were quite different from each other and lacked a clear through-line. To compile this section, the authors shared a conversation on Christmas Day of 2019 via KakaoTalk's Voice Talk [like Skype chat], from 8 to 10 pm, local time in Korea (GMT+9). Ji Kim then polished it up and put it into writing. There were broadly three topics in the discussion:

a) How they came to talk about K-pop and BTS in the first place; b) What BTS meant to them; c) Why Jane Do continued to remain blasé about K-pop and BTS. They also chatted at length about personal matters that most BTS fans would not care to hear. If you are still ok with this, please stick with us till the end.

지 킴 지금부터 두 사람이 얘기를 많이 하면 좋겠어. 뭐
든 이야기해도 좋아. 어쩌다 이 책에 참여하게 됐
는지 정도는 말해야겠지. 내 경우엔 이제 곧 마흔
이라 30대에 대한 기록을 남기고 싶었어. 그 안
에 케이팝이나 방탄소년단에 대한 흔적들이 있
어서 이걸 주제로 책을 내야겠다 했지. 생각해보
니 우리가 만난 지도 10년이 다 됐잖아. 우리 우정
의 기록물로 생각해도 좋겠다. 물론 두 사람에게
는 처음에 이건 대중서적이 될 거라고 그럴 듯하
게 말했지. 하지만 결국에는 세 사람의 사적인 이
야기 속에 방탄소년단이 언급되는 식이 돼버렸어.

Ji Kim So, I hope you girls will speak up.
Say whatever you like, but perhaps we can
start with how we all came to participate
in this book? For me, I will turn 40 in a few
years, and wanted to leave a record about

my 30s. And as my 30s has so many traces of K-pop and BTS, I thought it would be a great idea to write them down. Speaking of the passing of time, it's been almost 10 years since we first met. We can perhaps consider this as the record of our friendship, too? I know, I first sugar-coated it to you that this book would be for publication to the general public. But, in the end, it has become more a set of private stories that happen to mention BTS.

믹신 저는 언니가 쓰라고 해서 쓴 건데. (웃음) 저는 흔히 아미라고 말하는 방탄소년단의 팬과 팬덤에 대해 썼잖아요. 제가 어떻게 팬덤에 들어가게 됐고, 어떻게 받아들였으며, 어떤 식으로 그 안에서 덕질을 하는지. 글을 쓰기 시작하면서 깨달은 게 저는 이미 팬덤 안에 녹아 있어서 어떤 보편적인 시각으로 접근할 수가 없더라고요. 팬덤을 연구하는 문화연구 학자들 중엔 들뢰즈를 가져다 쓰기도 하고 팬덤의 다양한 모습을 관찰해 분석하기도 하던데, 저는 이미 팬의 입장이라 다르게 써야겠다 싶었어요. 뭐랄까, 한 개인의 서사에서 방탄소년단과 팬덤이 어떻게 등장하고 발전하는지 그 과정을 훑는 것도 좋지 않을까, 그런 생각으로 쓰게 됐는데 결과적으로는 팬덤 내에서 저는 어떤지, 어떤 위치인지를 역으로 정리하게 되더라고요.

Mick Shin Well, I wrote my essay because you made me (*laughs). I wrote about the BTS fandom we commonly refer to as ARMY. How I became to be part of the fandom, how I came to accept this, and how I geek out on BTS at the same time. What I realised when writing this essay was, I could not see BTS from a general, objective perspective, as I have internalised so much about the fandom already. I know there are a few cultural studies "scholars" who quote philosophers like Deleuze in the hope of understanding fandom, or seek to observe various dimensions of a fandom to yield a more dispassionate analysis. But I feel I am too much of a fan of BTS, so I thought I should approach this differently. Like, I thought it would be interesting to trace the genealogy of how BTS and fandom first appeared and have since developed in an individual's (my own) life story. That's how it started. But eventually I ended up finding out and reconfirming who I am and in what position I hold in this BTS fandom.

지킴 그리고 보니 우리 중 믹이 유일하게 팬으로서의 자신의 정체성을 고민하는 경우야. 어쩌다 팬이 된 거

였지?

Ji Kim Speaking of this fact, you are the only one among us pondering your own identity as a BTS geek, right? How did you become a BTS fan?

믹 신 제가 방탄소년단 팬이 된 이유는…. 예전에는 그랬어요. 가수나 배우, 어떤 스타를 좋아할 때, '저 사람 멋있다' 하고 동경하는 마음이 강했어요. 그런데 방탄소년단을 알고 난 후 느낀 건 새로운 감정이었어요. 함께 걸어서 좋은 그런 감정. 이 사람들이 조금 앞서나갈 때도 있지만 뒤돌아서 '같이 걷자' 하고 말 거는 느낌을 받았거든요. 저뿐 아니라 다른 팬들도 그렇게 느끼는 경우가 많더라고요.

Mick Shin I became a fan because… hmmm, in the past, when I liked a singer, actor, actress or any celebrity, I generally aspired to them, like, 'Wow they are amazing'. But for BTS, I feel somewhat different. I had a feeling that it's ok to walk with them "together". Sometimes they pass a few steps ahead of me, but then they keep turning around and telling me, "let's walk together". It's not just me but also some of other fans I know have the same feeling.

지킴 나도 믹과 비슷한 이유로 방탄소년단을 좋아하게 됐어. 런던에서 8년이라는 긴 시간을 보내면서 케이팝을 사람들이 어떻게 생각하는지 왕왕 들었거든. 싸이랑 빅뱅도 인기가 있었지만 방탄소년단을 기점으로 달라진 게, 사람들이 메시지에 주목하더라고. 방탄소년단은 좋은 음악만 만드는 게 아니라 유니세프와 같은 단체들의 사회적인 활동에도 참여하잖아. 좋은 일에 기부도 많이 하고. 그런데 영향을 받아서인지 팬들도 비슷한 활동들에 되게 열심인데, 그게 보도가 많이 됐어.

Ji Kim I think my reasons for liking BTS are similar to those of Mick. While I've been living in London for the past 8 years, I have come across other people's opinions on K-pop. PSY and Big Bang were pretty popular, but I think BTS was like a turning-point, from when people started paying attention to "messages". BTS not only make good music, they also participate actively in public activities of organisations like UNICEF. They also make quite a lot of donations. Perhaps what BTS do also inspires their fans, as they are quite active in public, communal activities, and the media have reported on them many times.

제인 도 영국에서?

Jane Do You mean, reported in the UK?

지킴 응, 영국의 〈메트로〉나 BBC 이런 유명 매체에서 여러 번 다뤘어. 그래서인지 방탄소년단과 그 팬덤에 대한 이미지가 정말 좋아. 물론 방탄소년단을 이런 이유로 우상화하거나 보통의 케이팝 밴드들과는 다르다고 주장하려는 건 아니야. 방탄소년단이 어떤 잘못도 안 할 리 없고 실제로 여러 논란에 휩싸인 거 잘 알고 있거든. 어떤 매체에 그에 대한 기사를 쓴 적도 있고. 그런데 말이지, 내가 방탄소년단을 계속 좋아하는 이유는 이후로 그런 잘못을 고치려고 노력하는 모습이 보이거든.

Ji Kim   Yes, and many times by "Metro", and even by famous media outlets like the BBC. Perhaps this is why BTS and their fandom have a good public image. I am not trying to idolise BTS for that reason, or suggesting they are qualitatively different from other K-pop bands. BTS do make mistakes, and I understand they have been caught up in several controversies. Some media sources reported on those issues, too. But nevertheless, I continue to like BTS as I can see they are trying to right the things they did wrong.

제인 도 이제 내 차례지? (웃음) 나는 방탄소년단의 팬은 아니지만 그에 대해 쓰고 싶은 이야기가 있었어. 어쨌든 나도 케이팝 현장에 있는 사람이라고 볼 수 있는데 이쪽 사람들이 케이팝이나 아이돌에 대해 발언할 때 그 내부보다는 표면적인 부분만 말하는 게 아쉬웠어. 피디들도 마찬가지라, "케이팝이 남미에서 인기가 많더라. 빨리 거기서 쇼를 해서 표 팔아 수익을 만들어 보자" 이런 식의 이야기를 아무렇지도 않게 하거든. 그리곤 실제로 해외로 가지. 그리고 카메라에 현지 팬들 반응을 비추면서 "이거 봐. 우리 케이팝이 이 멀리에서도 인기 있어" 그런 식으로 소위 말하는 한류의 이미지를 만

들려고 하거든. 현장에서 직접 그런 과정들을 보니까 오히려 난 그 한류라는 것의 진위가 궁금해지더라고. 진짜 실체가 있는 걸까.

Jane Do My turn, right? (*laugh*) I am not a BTS fan, but had a story that I wanted to pass on about them. I have somehow ended up working in the K-pop industry, but I'm a bit ashamed that so many people in this field tend to judge K-pop or K-idols by their looks rather than what's inside. This is even the same for many producers. "I heard K-pop is pretty sought-after in South America. Let's do a show there ASAP, sell tickets and make some money". These kinds of stories come out so casually. Then they actually go overseas. Then they show the local fans' reaction on screen and argue "Hey look, our K-pop is so popular in these far-off countries". They are trying to craft the reputation of the so-called Korean Wave. Having seen that process first hand has made me question the genuineness of the movement. Is it really a genuine thing?

지 킴 현장에 있는 네가 회의적으로 생각했다면 실체가 없었는지도 모르지.

Ji Kim If you are working on the spot and are sceptical like that, maybe it is not really genuine.

제인 도 산업적 측면에서 방송국 문제도 있는 게 우리나라 사람들은 외국인이 어떻게 받아들이냐 평가에 대해 민감한 편이잖아. 그래서인지 굳이 그렇게까지 할 필요 없는데 외국인 리액션을 의도적으로 더 많이 비춰. 한국에서 촬영을 할 때도, 내 눈엔

그게 어떤 면에선 작위적으로 느껴지거든. 근데 중요한 건, 방탄소년단을 보니까 해외에서 인기의 실체가 있긴 있더라고. 있었어. (웃음)

Jane Do　From an industrial perspective, broadcasters are partly responsible for this. You know, we Koreans are quite sensitive to evaluation by others, and how things are received by foreigners. Perhaps it's because of this they deliberately, if unnecessarily, show more reactions from non-Korean people, even when a show is taking place in Korea. To me, that somehow seems artificial. But you know what? BTS proves that the popularity of the Korean Wave is a real thing, really! (*laughs)

지 킴 아니, 왜 갑자기 돌변을. (웃음)

Ji Kim Why do you flip-flop your attitude so much? (*laughs)

제인 도 나중에 여행이나 시상식 참석하러 해외를 몇 번 나가게 됐는데 실제로 많은 사람이 케이팝에 반응을 하고 있더라고. 특히 방탄소년단에 대해서 이야기가 나오면 피부로 와 닿는 뜨거운 반응이 나왔어. (웃음) 그런 게 신기하면서도 동시에 이런 결론을 맺는 게 맞을까, 반신반의하게 되더라고. 방탄소년단의 성공을 부정하지 않지만, 그 성공을 미디어가 여전히 표피적으로 다루는데 여전히 거부감도 들고. 미디어가 말하지 않는 케이팝의 문제들을 이야기해보면 어떨까, 그런 생각으로 글을 썼어. 아이돌에 관심은 없지만 어쩌다 보니 연달아 아이돌이 나오는 프로그램을 맡게 돼 화면 뒤의 모습도 보게 되거든. 아이돌들이 정신적으로 힘들 수밖에 없는 산업의 구조적인 문제도 알게 돼. 그래서 나는 내 글에서 흥하는 케이팝, 방탄소년단의 성공만 이야기하고 싶지 않았어.

Jane Do Later I got a few chances to go abroad for travel or to attend some award ceremonies, and I saw how clearly the response that BTS won from the public. You know, when I started talking about them, I could feel people's enthusiasm in my bones (*laughs). That was quite magical, but I was not certain whether that should have been the conclusion of my essay. I don't deny the success of BTS, but I am also repulsed by the superficial and naïve ways in which the media present it. So, I thought, what if I write about the issues surrounding K-pop which the mainstream media does not address? That was my intention behind writing this essay. I am not interested in K-idols myself, but I have happened to be involved in producing programmes starring them and seeing the backstage processes that go on behind the screen. So, I was keen to learn more about the issues surrounding K-pop on a structural level, and what leads to the mental exhaustion of idol singers and groups. Seeing all this is what made me want to speak, not about the success of K-pop or BTS, but about the darker side.

믹 신 어떤 의미에서는 산업을 고발하는 글로 비춰질 수도 있는데 용감한 선택이었어요. 언니가 신변이 걱정돼 가명을 쓴다는 말을 처음에 듣곤 의아했는데 글을 읽으니까 그 이유를 알겠더라고요.

Mick Shin In some ways, your essay may appear to accuse the K-pop industry of certain wrongdoings, and I respect your boldness. I was a little puzzled when you said you were going to use a pseudonym because you were feeling uneasy about it, and now, having read your writing, I understand that.

제인 도 방송사에 있지만 이런 부분에 대해서 공식적으로 문제를 제기하기는 힘들어. 자리가 사람을 만들어서가 아니라, 어떤 일을 맡고 있느냐에 따라 발언권이 생기기도 없어지기도 하거든. 현실적으로 내가 맡은 역할에는 이런 문제에 대해 공식적으로 문제를 제기할 기회가 주어지지 않아. 갑자기 나서서 말한다 해도 들어주지 않지. 하지만 나는 진지하게 이런 문제들을 고민하고 있었고 이 글을 통해 내 솔직한 의견을 밝히고 싶었어.

Jane Do I work for a broadcaster, but it is still hard to bring these issues up formally. It is not because my position defines who I am, but because whether you have a voice depends on the type of work and position you undertake. In reality, in my case I have been given no chance to formally file complaints about these issues. And if you just interject a remark, people don't listen. But I have been mulling over these issues and wrestling with them in my mind, and I was looking for a chance to reveal my honest opinions.

지 킴 케이팝의 실체라고 하니까 하는 말인데, 나는 그냥 거리에서 본 경우잖아. 유학 오기 전부터 케이팝이 해외에서 인기 있다는 소리는 들었는데 솔직히 믿기진 않았어. 나도 기자로 일할 때 별 거 아닌 것도 어쩔 수 없이 별 거인 양 쓴 적 있었으니까. 런던에 와서 싸이 노래가 거리에서 흘러나올 때 놀라긴 했지. 그래도 잠깐일 거다, 그렇게 생각했거든. 왜 우리 어릴 때 들었던 '마카레나'처럼 잠깐 유행하고 말겠지, 영어도 아닌데 얼마나 듣겠어, 회의적이었던 거 같아. 그런데 내가 한국 사람이란 걸 알면 케이팝 이야기를 하는 사람들이 점점 생기더라고. 그래도 뭐, 나는 미디어 연구 쪽이니까 아무래도 내가 알게 되는 사람들은 한국뿐 아니라 다른 비서구권 문화에도 원래 관심을 가졌을 거야, 솔직히 그렇게 생각했어. 그런 식으로 아니지, 아닐 거야 하고 말이야. 그런데 방탄소년단이 나타나고는 그 케이팝의 실체라는 정말 있구나, 제인처럼 나 역시 느꼈어.

Ji Kim Speaking of the reality of K-pop, you know, all I know about it is what I have seen on the streets. Before I came to study abroad, I had heard about how K-pop was so popular overseas, and frankly, I didn't buy that. When I was working as a journalist before, I also hyped some stuff up, as that was my job. Yes, I was surprised when I found PSY's songs were playing on the street of London. But I thought it wouldn't last so long. Do you remember Los del Río's hit song "Macarena" when we were young? Just like that. Who would listen to a non-English song for long in the UK? I think I was doubtful. But then I started meeting a few people talking about K-pop when they found out I was from Korea. But still I went on like, 'Well, I research media, so the kind of people I get to know would already have had an interest, not just in Korean, but also other non-Western cultures'. But since BTS, I also felt the same as Jane. K-pop is a real thing!

믹 신 어떻게 다른데요? 영국에서의 방탄소년단에 대한
반응이 궁금했어요.

Mick Shin　What difference has BTS made,
do you think? I was dying to know about
public reactions to BTS in the UK.

지킴 내가 한정된 지면에 차마 다 쓸 수가 없었어. 내 이
야기만 하기도 했고. (웃음) 실은 일상적으로 방탄소
년단 팬들을 만나. 너무 많이. 예를 들어 내가 한국
학 가르치는 대학에 갈 때 기차를 타거든. 월요일마
다. 한 번은 내 뒷자리에서 방탄소년단 음악이 들리
더라고. 보니까 누가 봐도 영국 사람처럼 생긴 10대
후반쯤 돼 보이는 여자 분이 헤드폰으로 음악을 듣
고 있었어. 볼륨을 너무 높여 놔서 가는 내내 본의
아니게 〈Map of the Soul: Persona〉 앨범을 다 들
었네. 음. 또 다른 예는 뭐가 있을까. 옛날에 언론이
나 학계에서 말했던 걸 보면 케이팝이 해외에서 인기
있는 이유를 두고 폭력적이지 않고 섹스를 직접적으

로 다루지 않는 등 뭔가 건전한 콘텐츠로 소비돼서

래. 그래서 보수적인 국가들에서도 인기가 있다고.

Ji Kim I could not possibly write everything,
given the spatial constraint. Not to mention
the fact that I prioritised my own stories
(*laughs). Actually, I meet BTS fans in my
everyday life so often. For example, I take
the train to the university where I teach
Korean studies, every Monday. Once, I heard
BTS songs behind me. There was a teenage-
looking British girl listening to music on
her headphones. She had the volume
cranked up, so I had to listen to the entire
album of ⟨Map of the Soul: Persona⟩. Hmm,
what else. I heard through the grapevine
from some journalists and scholars that
K-pop is popular overseas in part because
they are consumed as a kind of healthy

cultural format that does not (directly) address violence or sex. That's why it is also so well received in some countries, where things are socially more conservative.

제인 도 그래. 그런 이야기 많았어.

Jane Do Yes, I've heard that too.

지 킴 하지만 내가 요즘 가르치는 아시아태평양학 전공 학생들을 보면 특정 인종이나 국적의 학생만 케이팝을 좋아하는 건 아니더라고. 대체로 케이팝에 관심이 많고. 설사 안 좋아하는 경우에도 방탄소년단은 다 알아. 어떤 학생이 나한테 그러더라, 방탄소년단은 '클래식'이라고. 그러다 보니 이미 영국에서는 케이팝이 일종의 대중문화 장르가 된 게 아닌가, 그런 생각마저 들 때가 있어. 한국에 대한 관심도 자연스레 늘어난 것도 같고. 얼마 전에는 런던에 있는 다른 학교에 일 보러 갔는데 복도에서 누가 "안녕하세요"

라고 한국어로 말을 거는 거야. 내가 "어떻게 한국어
를 배웠어요?"라고 영어로 물어보니까 케이팝 좋아
해서 조금 안대. 아, 방탄소년단 팬이라고도 그러더
라.

Ji Kim   But from the students majoring in
Asia-pacific related studies whom I've been
teaching these days, race or nationality
doesn't seem to determine their love for
K-pop. Generally they are interested in
K-pop, and even in cases when they are
not, everyone knows about BTS. One
student told me, BTS has become "classic".
So, sometimes it even occurs to me that
K-pop may now have become one of the
genres of popular culture in the UK. General
interests in South Korea also seemed to have
increased. A few days ago I went to another
university in London to run an errand, and

somebody spoke to me in Korean, "안녕하세요 [Hello in Korean]". I replied, in English, "How did you come to learn Korean?" and she said she knows a bit as she likes K-pop. Oh, and she's also a BTS fan.

제인 도 믹은 어땠어? 런던에서 열린 방탄소년단 콘서트 두 차례나 갔잖아. 현지 반응을 봤을 텐데.

Jane Do How about you Mick? You flew to London from Korea twice to attend BTS concerts there. You must've seen the vibe there?

믹 신 방탄소년단이 2019년 6월 1일과 2일, 이틀 동안 런던에서 콘서트를 했잖아요. 그래서 저도 갔죠. (웃음) 현장이 어땠냐면… 방탄소년단 팬의 연령층이 다양하다는 건 알고 있었지만 인종까지 다양할 줄은 몰랐었거든요. 아시아계가 많을 거라 예상했는데 딱히 그렇지도 않았어요. 백인, 흑인, 무슬림 모두 있더라고요. 그렇게 다양한 인종에서 10대, 20대 팬이 많이 왔던데, 제겐 그 점이 제일 놀라왔어요. 특히 10대 같은 경우에는 남에게 어떻게 보이느냐는 문제에 민감하잖아요. 문화 소비를 통해 정체성을 형성하는 나이대기도 하고요.

Mick Shin   Last year BTS held a two-day concert in London, from 1st to 2nd June. So I had no other choice but to go (*laugh). The vibe was… I knew that BTS have fans from all age groups, but I didn't know they also have fans from such a diversity of races and ethnicities. I assumed most of them would be Asians, but that was not really the case. There were many white people, black people, Arabic and Southeast Asian people, and so on. I was surprised especially by how most fans looked like teenagers or people in their 20s. I mean, teenagers are sensitive to how they appear to others, right? They are also in that period of life where they form identity through consuming cultural content.

제인 도 그때 누굴 좋아하느냐가 이성관이나 연애관에 영향을 끼치지….

Jane Do Who you like in that period does matter for your view of love and romance….

믹신 그니까요. 그런데 제가 20대에 런던에서 어학연수를 했을 때 직접 느낀 바로는 아시아 남성에 대한 부정적 인식이 꽤 있었거든요? 그런데 이번에 런던에 가보니 이럴 수가, 그 나이대 애들이 한국에서 온 아시안 보이밴드에 열광을 하는 거예요. 독특한 현상이 아닌가, 동시에 그 아이들이 주체적이다 생각했어요. 해외 웹사이트의 글을 보면 여전히 아시안 보이 밴드는 남성성 문제에서 폄하되는 경향이 있잖아요. 그런데 현장에서 본 10대 팬들은 방탄소년단을 좋아하는 자신을 거침없이 드러내더라고요. 그때 느낀 게 이 아이들도 나와 같은 게 아닐까. 방탄소년단과 방탄소년단의 팬으로서의 자신, 모두를 자랑스러워 하고 그 자체를 사랑하고 있다고요.

Mick Shin I know, right? But when I was in London in my 20s to study English, I sensed some negative stereotypes about Asian men. And now, my goodness. Teenagers were passionate about an Asian boy band from South Korea. That's quite something. At the same time, I thought they were self-determining. I still find on the Internet that somehow Asian boy bands tend to be belittled when it comes to the masculinity issue. But those teenagers I saw at the concert site were exhibiting their love of BTS outright. So I felt, maybe they are like me. We take pride in BTS and ourselves as BTS fans, and we like that fact.

지 킴 방탄소년단이 주는 메시지가 그런 정체성의 문제를 다루잖아. 앨범 제목만 봐도 네 스스로를 사랑하면 좋겠어. 어떻게 보면 진부하게 들릴 수도 있어. 하지만 중요한 이야기잖아. 무엇보다 다른 해외의 팝 밴드들은 그동안 그런 말을 안 했거든. 남녀 간의 사랑을 주로 이야기하지.

Ji Kim   BTS's messages deal with those kinds of identity issues for sure. Look at one of their album titles: ⟨(HOPE YOU) Love Yourself⟩. Perhaps it sounds lame. But it's important. Most overseas pop bands don't talk about loving yourself, only about the romantic love between men and women.

믹 신 제가 콘서트 기간 동안 묵은 호텔에는 한국 사람이 별로 없었어요. 숙박객 대부분이 방탄소년단 콘서트를 보러 유럽에서 온 사람들이었어요. 방탄소년단 캐릭터 인형이 달린 머리띠를 하고는 한 손에 응원 사인판을 들고 다른 한 손으로 아빠 손을 잡고 나서는 10대를 보고는, 뭐랄까, 이질적인 풍경이 맞는데 그 안의 사람에게서는 동질감을 찾게 되더라고요. 저는 한국인이고 방탄소년단을 한국 가수로 좋아한다고 생각했는데 런던에서 그런 경험들을 해보니 팬으로서 관점이 한층 넓어지는 것 같더라고요.

Mick Shin There were not many Koreans at the hotel where I stayed during the concert. It seemed most guests came from Europe to go to the BTS concert. Many teenagers were wearing BTS character headbands, holding cheer signs in one hand, their dad's hand in the other. This was somewhat strange, but

I got to find a sense of kinship with them nonetheless. I am Korean, and I had thought I liked BTS as a "Korean" singer, but this experience in London has broadened my perspective as a BTS fan.

●

제인 도 그처럼 인식이 바뀌게 된 데에는 방탄소년단이 달라진 것도 있지 않나. '케이팝 성공' 담론에 회의적인 나마저도 방탄소년단이 발전해 왔다는 걸 알겠거든. 어쩌다 보니 2015년 방탄소년단이 프로그램에 나와서 대면할 기회가 있었어. 당시에 어떤 가사들로 인해 여혐 논란이 있더라고. 개인적으로 그런 가사를 쓰는 아이돌을 좋아할 수는 없다고 생각했지. 하지만 어쨌든 일로 만났으니까 편견 없이 보려고 했지. 내 글이 케이팝이나 방송 산업에 대해 비판적이라 팬들이 어떻게 읽을지 미리 걱정이 되네. 사실 나 나중에 매니저랑 밥 먹으면서는 출연한 멤버들 칭찬했어. 특히 RM 말이야. 공부를 잘한다며. 그래서인가 말을 논리적으로 잘하더라. 뷔는 정말 순수해 보였어. 세상물정 모르는 게 아닌가 걱정이 들 정도로. (웃음)

Jane Do I think the shift in perception of Asian boy bands is also attributable to them being more mature. I still find dubious the "K-pop success" discourse, but then even I can see how they have grown. I happened to have the chance in 2015 to meet BTS, as they appeared on the show I produce. At that time, they were involved in a controversy surrounding misogyny in some of their lyrics. Personally, I felt I should not like boy bands who wrote those kinds of lyrics. But anyhow, we were meeting for business, so I tried to see them without any preconception. Now I am kinda anxious about how BTS fans might read my essay, as it is pretty critical of K-pop and the broadcasting industry. Actually, when I later had a chance to dine with their manager, I complimented the BTS members, especially RM. I heard he's smart. Actually he was an eloquent, cogent speaker. But V looked so innocent, almost naïve, that I was a little worried about him (*laughs).

지 킴 근데 말야. 생각해 보니 억울하네. 방탄소년단을 좋아하는 건 나랑 믹 둘인데 왜 니가 만난 거야. 정말 덕후는 계를 못 타는 거야? 특하나 그 파릇파릇할 때 말야. 분노가 치민다.

Ji Kim Speaking of meeting BTS, it's unfair

that you got to meet them whereas Mick and I never did, even though we are the BTS fans! Especially when they were in their springtime of life! Geeks are never blessed with these chances. I think I'm going to go and sulk.

제인 도 2017년에도 보긴 봤지. (웃음) 연말에 방송사에서 콘서트를 하잖아. 그때 잠깐 스치듯 봤는데 느낌이 확 달라졌더라고. 2년이라는 짧은 시간에 글로벌 스타로 성장했더라. 무대에서의 실력도 너무 달라져서 놀랐지. 내가 이전에는 미처 보지 못한 방탄소년단의 매력, 가치를 그 순간 느낀 것 같아. 하지만 뭐 이제 더는 못 볼 거야. 만날 수가 없거든. (웃음) 농담이 아니라 이제 영원히 못 만나지 않을까.

Jane Do   Well, I saw them again in 2017 (*laughs). You know, the broadcasting station I work for hosts an annual end-of-year concert. There I caught a glance at them and thought their image was much changed. In only two years, they had grown into global stars. I was surprised as well by how much their stage performance had improved. I think, at that moment, I became aware of BTS's real charm and value, in a way I hadn't noticed before. But I don't think I will see them again. There is no chance to meet people like this now (*laughs). It's no joke, I probably won't see them again forever!

지 킴 덕후가 아니라 또 만날 거야. 난 또 분노하겠지.

Ji Kim You aren't a BTS geek so you will probably meet them again one day. And I will fly into a rage again.

제인 도 팬은 계를 못 탄다고 하는데, 아니야. 내가 환상

을 확실히 깨주겠어. 예능 프로듀서라고 해서 연예인
과 일대일로 대화하거나 대면하는 일은 거의 없다시
피 하거든? 섭외나 대본 상의는 매니저 통해서 한다
고. 문제가 생겨도 매니저 통해 해야지 직접 가서 말
하면 난리 나요. 드라마 〈프로듀사〉에 나오듯이 직
접 가서 위로를 건네거나 하는 건 개뿔이야. 그런 걸
하는 사람은 이상한 피디예요. 진짜 이상한. (웃음) 팬
들에게처럼 그들은 나에게도 스타라고. 저 멀리서 지
켜볼 뿐이지.

Jane Do People say fans never get lucky,
but no. I will shatter your fantasy. Even if
you are an entertainment show producer,
you rarely get to meet or greet celebrities
in person. You liaise with them or discuss
the show scripts with their managers. When
you have any problems, you still bring it up
with their managers. If you take it directly
to the celebrities, you are seriously messing

things up. Yes, in the TV drama ⟨The Producers⟩, some producers offer words of encouragement to the stars, but that's just bullsh*t. Whoever actually does that is a weirdo, really bizarre (*laughs). Just like with their fans, they are stars to me too. I watch them from afar.

지 킴 사인 CD는 받잖아요.

Ji Kim At least you get signed CDs.

제인 도 CD 받는 것도 어렵다고요. 방탄소년단은 한국에 잘 오지 않잖아. 잠깐 와도 짧게 활동하고, 주로 활동할 때 CD를 돌리는데 그때 자리 안 지키면 못 받지.

Jane Do Not really, that's not easy either. BTS are not in Korea that often, and when they are, they just stay for a week or so for their entertainment business. That's when they hand out signed CDs but you have to be actually there on site to get them.

지 킴 자리에 항상 있어야지. 자리를 지켜야 우리도 구경이라도 하지.

Ji Kim So, be on your spot all the time. You stay at your spot and that's how we can at least see the BTS-signed CDs.

제인 도 일은 안 해? (웃음)

Jane Do Stay on the spot all the time and don't work? (*laughs)

믹 신 언니 아는 분은 저번에 사인 CD 받고 분실했다고 하지 않았어요? 방탄소년단 팬에게 보냈는데 중간에 사라졌다고?

Mick Shin Didn't you say that one of your

acquaintances lost a CD last time? That you sent over it to a BTS fan and it somehow disappeared on the way?

제인 도 내가 아는 선배 프로듀서가 두바이에서 일하는 친구한테 어렵게 구한 방탄소년단 사인 CD를 보낸 거야. 근데 중간에 사라졌어. 택배로 가는 과정에서 누가 상자를 뜯고 훔쳐갔대.

Jane Do Yes, a senior producer I know sent over to her friend working in Dubai some BTS-signed CDs she had managed to scrape together. But they vanished when being delivered by courier. Apparently someone tore open the parcel and stole them.

믹 신 인기가 정말 장난이 아니구먼요.

Mick Shin They really are tremendously popular.

지 킴 제인 말에 공감하게 되는 게, 맞아. 생각해 보니까 나도 기자로 일할 때 감독이나 배우를 주로 인터뷰 하니까 부러워하는 친구들이 있었거든. 내가 일한 데는 잡지라서 보통 일대일로 만나 한두 시간 정도 제한된 시간 내에 인터뷰를 하지. 하지만 그런 인터 뷰마저 하기 전이나 후에 다 '세팅'이 된다고. 미리 질 문지 보내달라는 사람도 있고 인터뷰 중간이나 끝 나고 나서도 기껏 말한 것도 '오프 더 레코드'로 해 달라고 부탁해.

Ji Kim   I think I sympathise with Jane. Thinking about it, I also had a few friends who were jealous of me when I was working as a journalist and interviewing film directors or actors. I was working for a film magazine and meeting with them for face-to-face interviews for a limited time; like an hour or two. But those interviews are sort of pre-structured and pre-configured.

Some people ask for the interview questions
in advance, others ask in the middle of the
interview or after interview that they want
"off-the-record" for things they just said.

제인 도 그래 니가 그런 문제로 초반에 힘들어 했었지.
Jane Do That's right. You had a hard time
because of those issues.

지킴 나는 되게 평범하고 야망이 없는 기자였기 때문에
영화나 드라마에서 나오는 것처럼 허를 찌르는 질
문으로 특종 기사를 내보자, 그런 욕심을 부린 적도
없었지. (웃음) 혹 민감한 주제를 다룬다고 해도 뒷수
습은 어떻게 할 거야. 그 배우의 기획사나 감독의 제
작사랑 영원히 안 보고 살 거 아니잖아. 업계가 작거
든. 한 페이지짜리 짧은 인터뷰에도 기획사, 광고주,
잡지사의 이해관계가 복잡하게 얽혀 있는데 그런 걸
다 무시하고 쓸 수 없지. 어떤 때는 내가 쓰는 기사

가 상품처럼 느껴지기도 했어. 하지만 내가 제인과
다르게 생각하는 건, 방탄소년단은 말이지. 내가 팬
이라서 하는 말이 아니라 다른 거 같아. 보통 상품이
라고 말하는 아이돌 밴드들과 소통 방식이 달라.

Ji Kim I was just a run-of-the-mill journalist
with little ambition, so I was never eager to
bite off more than I could chew, like asking
a shrewd question to get a scoop like in the
films or TV shows (*laughs). Had I dealt with
some sensitive topics, I would've had no idea
how to mop something like that up. It's not
like I will never see the actors again, their
agencies or the people like film directors
and production companies. It's a small
world. Even writing a one-page interview
had to take into account the complex
interests of actors' agencies, advertisers,
sponsors, and the magazine I was working

for. Sometimes, I felt my articles were a commodity. But my opinion is somewhat different from yours, Jane, regarding BTS. I'm not saying this just because I'm a fan of theirs, but also, I feel something is different. Their modes of communication are unlike those of other idol bands we liken to commodities.

제인 도 예를 들면? 어떤 점에서 그렇다는 건데?

Jane Do For instance? In what way?

지 킴 방탄소년단은 소셜 미디어로 팬들과 직접 대화하거든. 나도 가끔 브이앱을 보는데 볼 때마다 놀래. 이건 비나 싸이 같은 이전 세대는 절대 할 수 없는 거야. 제인이나 내가 일할 땐 그 산업 내부에서 수십 년동안 축적해 놓은 노하우로 만들어 놓은 포맷을 따랐잖아. 그런 포맷을 통해 스타로서의 이미지를 만

들고 그에 맞춰 전략적으로 스스로를 노출해 온 이
전의 세대들은 그런 소셜 미디어의 쌍방향성에 적응
하기가 힘들 거야. 브이앱에서 방탄소년단 멤버들을
보면 직접 내러티브를 만들거든. 어떤 산업이 도저
히 만들거나 조작할 수 없는 진정성authority이 있을
수밖에 없지. 그런 점에 나는 매번 놀라는 거야. 더
좋아지고.

Ji Kim BTS directly converse with their fans
through social media. I also watch the V
Live app sometimes, and every time I do, I
am quite amazed. Previous generations of
K-pop entertainers and singers, like Rain
or PSY, would never have been able to do
the same. You know, when Jane or I are at
work, we normally follow certain "formulae"
that have been established based on know-
how accumulated over time in the industry.
That's the same for the previous generation's

K-pop entertainers: they built their profiles as stars through certain verified formulae and organised their representation in a very strategic way accordingly. These people would find it hard to adapt themselves to this bidirectionality and the interactiveness of social media. On V Live, BTS members make up their own narratives, so there is a sense of authenticity that cannot be fabricated or manipulated by the industry. I am startled by this. And they get better and better.

제인 도 방탄소년단은 그런 내러티브뿐만 아니라 가사도 직접 쓰잖아. 그런 진정성 있는 스토리들에 팬들이 감정을 이입하게 되고 그 과정에서 방탄소년단과 더 끈끈하게 결속될 수 있겠어. JYP 출신의 A&R 담당 자를 만난 적이 있는데 비슷한 이야기를 하더라. 팬

들은 방탄소년단이 주는 메시지들의 의미를 정확히
알고 있다. 1집에서 2집, 2집에서 3집으로 어떻게 내
러티브가 변화하는지, 각각은 어떤 이야기를 들려주
는지 간파한대. 그렇게 서로 메시지를 주고받는 사
이라면 단단해질 수밖에 없지. 방탄소년단과 팬덤의
관계가 공고한 건 그래서인가봐.

Jane Do They make their own narratives
but also write lyrics themselves, right? Fans
must empathise with those kinds of bona
fide stories, it will help them to feel more
intimately connected. I have heard a similar
story from an A&R person from JYP: "BTS
fans understand exactly the meaning of
messages from BTS. They grasp how BTS'
stories have changed from the first album to
the second, from the second to the third, and
so on, trying to figure out what each story is
about". These kinds of reciprocal exchange

and understanding must strengthen the relationship. Perhaps that's why BTS and BTS fandom have such a solid connection.

지 킴 내가 가장 좋아하는 멤버는 지민이지만 제이홉이 하는 브이앱을 더 잘 찾아봐. 제이홉은 정말 너무 귀여워. 인간적으로 너무 매력이 넘치는데, 뭣보다 자신을 있는 그대로 솔직하게 드러내거든. 채팅창의 팬들 반응도 주의 깊게 보면서 일상적으로 대화하듯 그렇게 자기 삶을 잘 보여줘. 정이 안 갈 수가 없지.

Ji Kim   My favourite BTS member is Jimin, but I watch J-Hope's channel on V Live more often. J-Hope is so adorable. He has a lot of personal charms, and most of all, he really opens himself up candidly. He pays careful attention to the fans' reactions on chatrooms and reveals the details of his daily life. How can you not feel attached to him?!

제인 도 빅히트 이전의 거대 기획사들은 확실히 자기 스타들이 말실수를 할까 봐, 혹 기획사가 정해놓은 캐릭터나 이미지에서 맞지 않는 발언을 할까 봐 전전긍긍 하는 게 있어. 빅히트는 그런 걸 제지하지 않은 거지. 자기 스스로를 드러내고 적극적으로 소통했다는 점에서 방탄소년단은 동년배 밴드들과도 달랐던 거 같아. 중소돌로 시작했으니 그게 하나의 생존전략이 었을 수도 있고. 문제는 덕분에 방송국에서 방탄소년단을 볼 수 없게 됐다는 거지. 예능이 필요하지 않은 스타니까. (웃음)

Jane Do It's true that large entertainment agencies before Big Hit felt some trepidation about their stars making blunders, unleashing Freudian slips, or saying something that did not go along with their pre-determined persona or public image. But Big Hit did not hold them back. They opened themselves up and communicated actively - that's how they differentiated themselves from other bands of the same generation. Perhaps that's one of their survival strategies, given they were not part of the three major entertainment agencies (SM, YG, JYP). One problem now is, we can no longer see them at broadcasting stations. They are superstars who no longer need to appear on TV entertainment shows (*smiles).

믹신 소셜 미디어라는 게 되게 위험할 수도 있거든요. 하지만 요즘 소비자는 소셜 미디어에 익숙해서 그 안의 가짜와 진짜 정도는 구별할 수 있다고 봐요. 방탄소년단이 데뷔한 지 7년 됐거든요. 만약 그 공간에서 팬들을 속이거나 본인인 아닌 모습을 작위적으로 보여줬다면 분명 그에 대한 말이 나왔을 거예요.
그런데 팬들은 오히려 그 과정에서 이들이 발전하는
모습을 봤다고 하거든요. 적어도 저는 그랬어요. 요
즘 팬덤은 거짓은 가릴 줄 아는 현명한 소비자이고
스스로도 그렇다고 생각하는데, 방탄소년단에 대해
서는 거짓이 아니라는 믿음이 있어요.

Mick Shin Social media can be something
really dangerous. But I think today's
consumers are more familiar with social
media and can distinguish between what's
fake and what's real. BTS debuted seven
years ago. If they have deceived their fans or
artificially made up what they are for those
years, then that surely would have emerged.
But fans are convinced they have seen how
BTS have grown, for real. At least I am. I
consider myself as a sensible consumer
who can discern truth from falsehood, and

I believe BTS are neither bogus nor two-faced.

지 킴 나도 믿어. 내게 방탄은 진짜고 진실이야. 아니라면 이 책을 시작할 수 없었을 거야.

Ji Kim I share the same belief. To me, BTS is genuine and real. Otherwise I could not have started this book.

제인 도 둘한테 항상 그랬지. 나는 팬이 아니라고, 그래도 괜찮냐고. 그런데 이상하지, 쓰다 보니 방탄소년단에 입문했다는 기분이 들어.

Jane Do I used to tell both of you, I am not a BTS fan, and are you ok with that. But it's odd, with writing, I now feel like I am introduced to BTS.

지 킴 좋은 게 좋은 거지. 그거야말로 이 글을 읽는 독자들이나 방탄소년단 팬들이 가장 바랄 결론일 거야. 나름 해피엔딩이네.

Ji Kim   Well - all's well that ends well. Probably that's the conclusion our readers or BTS fans would like to hear the most. All in all, it's a happy ending!

주

1 Jenkins, H. (2008). 팬, 블로거, 게이머: 참여 문화에 대한 탐색 (정
   현진 역). 비즈앤비즈. (원서 출판 2006).

2 영국의 일간지인 〈데일리 메일〉(Daily Mail)은 2018년 10월 12일,
   지민의 스물세 번째 생일을 축하하기 위해 중국 팬커뮤니티인 지민
   바 차이나(Jiminbar China)가 런던의 엔젤역을 비롯해 미국 뉴욕
   의 타임즈 스퀘어와 네덜란드 암스테르담에 위치한 대형 경기장인
   지고돔의 빌보드 광고판을 빌렸다고 보도했다.

3 지민바 차이나는 해마다 지민의 생일을 기념하는 대형 이벤트를 기
   획한다. 이 팬클럽이 2019년 주최한 다른 행사들은 다음의 기사를
   참고할 것
   한정원 (2019). 방탄 지민 中 초대형 생일 이벤트, 45개 도시 2,629
   스크린 동시 진행, 뉴스엔, 8월 29일

4 지민의 국내 팬클럽인 올포지민코리아(All for Jimin Korea)에서
   지난 2019년 10월에 있었던 지민의 생일을 축하하기 위해 벌인 행
   사들은 그 트위터 계정인 @ALLFORJIMIN_KOR에 자세하게 소
   개돼 있다.

note

1 Jenkins, H., 2006. Fans, Bloggers, and Gamers: Media
   Consumers in a Digital Age. New York, NY: New York
   University Press.

2 Rabinovich, B., 2018. 'BTS's Jimin's birthday project: Fans
   celebrate with billboards in New York and Amsterdam',
   Daily Mail [online], 12 October.

3 For details of the events 'Jimin Bar China' have organised
   in 2019, see the following hyperlink (in Korean):
   https://newsen.com/news_view.php?uid=20190829115
   5186210

4 For details of the events "All for Jimin Korea" organised
   to celebrate Jimin's birthday in October 2019, see
   @ALLFORJIMIN_KOR on Twitter.

5 For a detailed discussion of 'hybridization' and
   'media hybrid' as the next stage in the evolution

5 레프 마노비치는 〈소프트웨어가 명령한다〉(2013)에서 '미디어 혼종
화'의 개념을 새롭게 제시했다. 그에 따르면 기존의 모든 미디어 테
크놀로지를 소프트웨어로 전환하는 미디어의 '소프트웨어화'가 이
루어진 후 그 생산물의 특징도 혼종적으로 변화했다.
Manovich, L. (2014). 소프트웨어가 명령한다 (이재현 역). 커뮤니
케이션북스. (원서 출판 2013).

6 마르셀 모쓰의 증여론에 관심이 있다면 2002년에 영문판으로 출간
된 〈The Gift〉를 읽어볼 것
Mauss, M. (2002). The gift: The form and reason for
exchange in archaic societies. Routledge.

7 방탄소년단이 한국 사회에서 터부시되는 주제들, 즉 성 소수자 권
리, 정신 건강, 성공에 대한 압박 등을 어떻게 다루는지에 대해서는
아래 〈롤링스톤즈〉의 기사를 참고할 것
Kim, J. H. (2018). 'How BTS Are Breaking K-Pop's Biggest
Taboos', Rolling Stone [online], 29 May.

8 방탄소년단이 유니세프와 손을 잡고 시작한 '엔드바이올런
스'(#END violence) 캠페인은 전 세계 어린이와 10대들에 대한 폭
력에 반대하는 운동을 조직적으로 펼치기 위해 기획됐다.

of computational media and 'cultural species', see Manovich, L., 2013. Software Takes Command. New York, NY: Bloomsbury Academic.

6   For those interested in Marcel Mauss' gift theory, see: Mauss, M., 2002. The Gift: The form and reason for exchange in archaic societies. London: Routledge.

7   Kim, J. H., 2018. 'How BTS Are Breaking K-Pop's Biggest Taboos', Rolling Stone [online], 29 May.

8   BTS has joined hands with the United Nations Children's Fund to stage campaigns against violence towards children and teens around the world (#END violence).

9   Kim, C.-S, 2019. 'BTS RM donated 100 million Korean won to special school for the deaf for music education', Yonhap News [online], 20 September.

10 Kim, J.-S, 2019. 'BTS J-Hope made 100 million Korean won donation on his birthday', JoongAng Ilbo [online], 18 February.

9 김철선 (2019). '방탄소년단 RM, 청각장애학교에 1억 기부...음악교육에 써달라', 연합뉴스, 9월 20일

10 김진석 (2019). '방탄소년단 제이홉, 생일 맞아 1억 원 기부', 중앙일보, 2월 18일

11 n.a. (2019). '방탄소년단 슈가, 팬클럽 이름으로 소아암 환아들에 1억 원 기부', 동아일보, 3월 9일

12 황혜진 (2019). '방탄소년단 제이홉 팬들 급다른 기부, 나눔의집 →53개 국 기아 후원 캠페인', 뉴스엔, 2월 17일

13 〈메트로〉는 이 기사에서 지민의 팬클럽이 보인 선행을 두고 "Mad respect"라고 코멘트를 남겼다.

14 〈번 더 스테이지〉는 유튜브 레드 오리지널 시리즈로, 〈2017 BTS Live Trilogy Episode III: The Wings Tour〉 300일간을 다큐멘터리 형식으로 기획해, 총 8편(편당 약 30분)으로 만들어졌다. 투어는 19개 도시 총 40회 공연으로 55만 명의 관람객을 동원했다.

15 유튜브 레드는 광고 없이 유튜브 영상을 시청할 수 있는 유료 서비스다. 2015년 10월 미국에서 처음 서비스를 출시했으며, 한국에서

11 'n.a., BTS Sugar donated 100 million Korean won to childhood cancer patients, in the name of his fan club', Dong-a Ilbo [online], 9 March.

12 Hwang, H. -J., 2019. 'BTS J-Hope's fans' donation is in a different league, including a nursing home for living comfort women and supporting child poverty in 53 countries', Newsen [online], 17 February.

13 Besanvalle, J., 2019. 'Over 600 BTS fans donate blood in Korea in honour of Jimin's 24th birthday', Metro [online], 13 October.

14 YouTube Red Originals. The documentary of 300-day tour ⟨2017 BTS Live Trilogy Episode III: The Wings Tour⟩.

15 A paid streaming subscription service that provides advertising-free streaming of all videos hosted by YouTube.

16 Often referred to as "V App", V Live app is a South

는 2016년 12월부터 서비스를 시작했다.

16 브이앱은 포털 사이트 네이버에서 서비스하는 글로벌 스타 인터 넷 방송 플랫폼이다. 2015년 9월 1일에 공식 오픈했다. 'V Live 앱' 을 줄여서 브이앱이라고 흔히 불린다. 2020년 2월, 방탄소년단의 브이앱 채널 팔로워는 1,700만 명을 넘어섰다.

17 2018년 8월 서울에서 시작하여 2019년 4월까지 20개 도시 42회 공연으로 총 104만 명의 관객을 불러 모았다. 2019년 5월 미국 로 즈볼 스타디움을 시작으로 〈Love Yourself: Speak Yourself〉 스타디움 투어를 진행하였고, 그해 10월 29일 서울 올림픽 스타디 움에서 투어의 마지막을 장식했다. 이 스타디움 투어는 10개 도시 20회 공연으로 102만 명의 관객이 관람했다.

18 메이크업 하는 한국 남성에 대한 BBC의 기사는 다음을 참고. n.a. (2018). 'Flowerboys and the appeal of 'soft masculinity' in South Korea', BBC, 5 Sep.

19 White Paper Project의 웹사이트는 서버 이전 과정에서 발생한 문제들을 해결하기 위해 2019년 12월부터 닫혀 있는 상태다.

20 앙드레 지드의 소설 〈좁은 문〉의 '좁은 문에 이르길 힘쓰라'는 성경

Korean live video streaming service owned by Naver Corporation.

17 〈BTS World Tour: Love Yourself〉 began on the 25th of August 2018 in Seoul, South Korea. The tour was extended with a separate title: 〈BTS World Tour - Love Yourself: Speak Yourself〉, which began in Pasadena, California in May 2019, and concluded on the 29th of October 2019 in Seoul.

18 For the BBC's article on Korean men wearing makeup, see the following hyperlink: https://www.bbc.co.uk/news/world-asia-42499809

19 We are a group of BTS fans who believe firmly in the power of knowledge and discussion. We hope that our product will help bring light to aspects of this event that were left unexplored, and help contribute to a more nuanced understanding of the complexity of intercultural relations and transmedia communications in East Asia and beyond. [Excerpt from White Paper Project website]

속 마태복음의 한 구절이다.

Gide, A. (2013). 좁은 문 (이성복 역). 문학과 지성사. (원서 출판 1909).

21 〈80년생 김지영〉은 조남주 작가가 쓴 소설로 출간 2년 만에 100만 부가 판매됐다. 1982년 서울에서 태어난 김지영의 생애를 통해 한국에서 여성으로 산다는 것이 어떤 것인지 조명했다. 영화로도 제작돼 350만 명 이상의 관객이 들었다.

이은호(2019). [이은호의 문화 ON] 영화 '82년생 김지영' 흥행 비결, 쿠키뉴스, 12월 9일

22 2015년에 방영된 드라마로 KBS 예능국을 배경으로 펼쳐지는 이야기를 다뤘다. 버라이어티 프로그램 피디, 음악방송 피디, 신입 피디와 아이돌 밴드 출신의 여자 가수가 주요 등장인물이다.

23 윤가은은 2016년 영화 〈우리들〉로 장편 데뷔를 한 영화감독이다. 2019년 작품인 〈우리집〉도 아역 배우들이 주요 인물이다. 이 책에서 언급한 촬영 수칙은 〈우리집〉 촬영 당시 윤 감독이 고안한 것.

이서현 (2019). '보람TV도 참고해야 할 영화 '우리집'의 '어린이 촬영 수칙', 동아일보, 8월 14일

C.f., White Paper Project website is under extended maintenance to fix issues occurred during the server relocation process.

20 An excerpt from French author André' Gide's "Strait is the Gate". Originally recorded in the Gospel of Matthew in the Holy Bible.

21 ⟨Kim Ji-young, Born 1982⟩ is a million-selling fiction novel by Cho Nam-joo, first published in October 2016. It depicts the everyday sexism a housewife named Kim Ji-young has experienced since youth.

22 ⟨The Producers⟩ is a Korean drama that narrates the story of the dynamic work and life of a celebrity singer and producers working in the KBS's entertainment division.

23 A South Korean film director who explores the stories of young children and youth. The above rules were devised during the filming of ⟨The House of Us⟩ (2019).